Nothing Up My Sleeve but Pixie Dust

How Working at Disneyland's Main Street Magic Shop Changed Everything

Nothing Up My Sleeve but Pixie Dust:
How Working at Disneyland's Main Street Magic Shop
Changed Everything

Lambert Hill, 371A Oak Place, Brea, CA 92821
Books@LambertHill.com

ISBN: 9781737428503

This book is a memoir. The work depicts actual events in the life of
the author as truthfully as recollection permits or can be verified
through research. Although every effort has been made to ensure
that the information is correct, the author and publisher assume no
responsibility for errors or omissions, and disclaim all liability to any
loss, damage, or disruption caused by the information contained
herein. The views expressed are those of the author alone.

This book is not authorized by, endorsed by, or associated with
Disneyland Park, The Walt Disney Company, Disney Enterprises,
Inc., or any of their subsidiaries or affiliates. All references made to
these company's copyrights, trademarks and registered marks are
used in accordance with the Fair Use Doctrine and are not meant to
imply this book is a Disney product for advertising or other
commercial purposes.

To
The young at heart:
May Never Land be forever in your sights.

Nothing Up
My Sleeve but
Pixie Dust

How Working at Disneyland's Main Street
Magic Shop Changed Everything

A Memoir

By
Bruce Edwards

Lambert Hill

The author performs his favorite vanishing coin trick.

Contents

Introduction

To all those who have ever been to Disneyland, you're surely familiar with Peter Pan's Flight—the Fantasyland ride that sails you over the moon, to a land where you never grow up. What you probably didn't know is that a *second* Never Land exists in the park, where aging is optional. It's a little treasure tucked away on Main Street, U.S.A.: The Main Street Magic Shop.

For the "lost boys" who worked there in the 1970s, fun and mischief were the orders of the day. I know, because I was privileged to be one of them. If you've ever wondered what it was like to be part of that tomfoolery, here's your chance to find out. Enjoy the view from behind the counter, as I reveal my personal account of what made that little shop so extraordinary.

Since its opening in 1957, the shop's main attraction has been watching real magicians perform amazing tricks. But if you were lucky, you might also become the target of one of their hilarious gags. Meet those unpredictable cast members who brought laughter to spectators and victims alike. Learn the answer to burning questions, such as: How many springs can you fit in one snake can? Did you really hang rubber spiders from strings to scare people? How often did your supervisors cut them down?

How I came to work there is a tall tale in itself. Growing up in mid-century America, kids like me were thoroughly enchanted by Walt Disney's ingenuity. His inventiveness inspired me to embark on a creative journey of my own. Little did I know that road would lead me to Walt's landmark creation. Join me as I retrace my steps from small-town dreamer to Disneyland contributor.

Though I primarily examine the silliness the Magic Shop was known for, this is not just a collection of funny stories. It's a peek behind the curtain at the ins and outs of running a Disneyland shop. Discover how personalities and points of view sometimes collided, just like they do in any other workplace. But mostly, it's a tribute to what made working at The Happiest Place on Earth so special.

For some of you, reliving these moments will rekindle fond memories. Baby Boomers will enjoy revisiting a time before smart phones and social media. All are welcome. So, grab a handful of pixie dust and come fly with me, to a world of magic and wonder. Or, as Peter Pan likes to say: "C'mon, everybody. Here we gooooo!"

—Bruce Edwards, 2021

Chapter 1
Land of Dreams

"I want always to be a little boy and to have fun."
—Peter Pan

It was a sight I will never forget. Riding south on Interstate-5 in 1963, with Mom, Dad and older brothers Phil and Bob, we had just crossed the Anaheim, California city limits. It had been a 400-mile trek from Marin County, up north. On a freeway billboard, the Seven Dwarfs informed us that Disneyland was only 3 miles ahead. I was already teetering on the edge of madness, anticipating our family's vacation at the Happiest Place on Earth, when out from behind the billboard appeared the snow-capped summit of Matterhorn Mountain! Seeing the iconic structure rising out of that suburban landscape was odd to say the least. To a 12-year-old boy like me, it was nothing short of magical.

Disney Magic is a common term used to describe Walt's knack for bringing so much joy to so many. Disneyland is the prime example of this, although it took more than a little *abracadabra* to pull it off. Shortly after its 1955 opening, critics pronounced that the park had little hope of long-term success. And yet, nearly 70 years later, the Matterhorn stands as a testament to Walt's vision and persistence.

This was not my first trip to Disneyland, nor would it be my last. There were actually four significant dates upon which that enchanted land would impact my life. The first was my maiden visit in 1957. The last would find me greatly extending my stay, becoming a park cast member.

This may sound a little far-fetched, but I can trace Walt Disney's influence on me back to my toddler years. The animated feature *Peter Pan* had just been released to theaters, and my parents brought me along to see it. Being only 2 years old at the time, recalling my initial reaction is somewhat fuzzy. My memory of the film's flying sequences, however, is crystal clear. My jaw must have been on the floor watching Wendy, John and Michael fly over London. All these years later, in my sleep I see myself beside them, soaring high above the clouds. I call these my "multiplane" dreams, due to another Disney innovation called the Multiplane Camera, which renders animation with astounding realism.

In our household, going to the movies wasn't just something to do on a Saturday night. It was a major event. Mom would get all dressed up and Dad put on a tie. Then we'd all pile into the car and drive in to San Francisco, to soak up that movie palace experience. Since we rarely ventured outside our hometown of Novato, these were our more extravagant outings. We were not a highbrow family, and found entertainment in the simplest of activities. I still remember the thrill we shared, riding to the top floor in our town's new 2-story office building elevator.

Like most suburbanites in the 1950s, we rarely worried about security. You left your car keys in the ignition while shopping, unafraid that someone might steal your car. Back doors were left unlocked when you went on vacation, allowing neighbors access to feed your cat while you were away. In the event you needed the services of law enforcement, help was just a phone call away.

Not everyone in town owned a phone, but we did. Interestingly, there were no numbers on the dial. To make a call you lifted the receiver, then gave the operator the two-letter, one-digit number of the party you wanted to reach.

Though our middle-class existence was a modest one, we didn't want for basic necessities. Still, we were ever mindful of our limited budget. We didn't splurge on items we didn't need. Why waste money on an electric dishwasher when you have running water, soap and a dish rack?

But there was one luxury we simply couldn't do without. We ordered a TV antenna strapped to our chimney, to matched the hundreds of others that sprouted from rooftops all over town. A wire through a cracked-open window fed broadcast signals to our living room TV set. Through that black and white screen I discovered the world Walt Disney had created. Each day after school I ran home to catch *The Mickey Mouse Club*. To miss a single episode of *The Adventures of Spin and Marty* was inexcusable. At my tender age, I wasn't mature enough to appreciate Annette's blossoming into adolescence. What intrigued me more was Cubby O'Brian's skill at playing the drums.

One of my other Disney favorites was *The Adventures of Zorro*. The title character's signature was slashing the letter Z on everything from drapes to wanted posters to the seat of Sergeant Garcia's pants. For those wishing to emulate that afternoon TV idol, toy makers came up with a plastic sword for kids. The tip of it held a piece of chalk, allowing young fans to swish Zs harmlessly around the house. I didn't own that coveted plaything, yet was determined to leave Zorro's calling card no matter what. In grandiose fashion, I swished Zs all over the walls of my bedroom, as if the hand of Guy Williams (who played Zorro) was guiding my every movement. There was only one problem: unable to lay my hands on a piece of chalk, I used an indelible marker instead!

This was in no way retaliation for being denied that play sword. I just didn't know any better. Happily, I was not reprimanded for my act of empty-headedness. My folks were fully aware of the impact Disney was having on my upbringing. A few yards of wallpaper and the whole incident was forgotten.

Television wasn't the only medium through which I consumed Disney Magic. I listened to 78 rpm records on our phonograph. For hours I'd sit on the living room rug and follow the exploits of *The Three Little Pigs*, or listen to Basil Rathbone narrate *The Adventures of Mr. Toad*.

Our home library held a respectable collection of Little Golden Books. These mostly related the stories from Disney's short films, like *Bongo, Little Toot* and *Johnny Appleseed*. Our Big Golden Books were more colorful adaptations of Walt's feature films: *Dumbo, Bambi,* and of course, *Peter Pan*.

While my generation looked to Walt for fun and entertainment, parents appreciated the wholesome nature of his work. Raising children on Disney values helped teach kids the rules of decency and respect. This did not always guarantee that every child got the message. When I was in kindergarten, I watched our teacher wash a boy's mouth out with soap for speaking an obscene word. (Today that would surely be grounds for legal action.)

But then, post-war kids weren't terribly bright. Catch reruns of Art Linkletter's afternoon TV shows from that period and see for yourself. Art was best known for interviewing young children on camera. They were asked questions only grownups could answer. Work and dating were frequent topics. Having little knowledge of such matters, the candid remarks these youngsters gave had audiences howling with laughter. Kids today are far more articulate. They can speak on the issues of the day as well as anyone. Why? Either all that time they spend on line has smartened them up, or school teachers are doing a better job than we give them credit for.

I was still years away from reaching that level of competence. But despite my minor league brainpower, I was bursting with creativity. I spent most of my playtime drawing, thanks in large part to the Walter Foster books we owned—two of which provided instruction on how to animate cartoon characters. I studied them intensely.

Copying the drawings into flip books allowed me to watch my crude artwork come to life. I daydreamed of someday entering the field of animation professionally. As encouragement, my folks bought me *The Art of Animation* by Bob Thomas, a colorful book which reveals how the Disney artists created those amazing animated films. To this day, that precious volume holds a place of honor on my book shelf.

My dad had an interesting theory on creativity. He believed that creative thinking was a kind of spiritual exercise. Most neuroscientists agree that the human brain is little more that a biological computer. It merely absorbs input through the physical senses, and has no more creative ability than a printed circuit board. All original ideas that have ever been, or are yet to be imagined, are already out there. All you have to do is be receptive to them. Think about it. You say, "I *came up* with an idea." You *find* inspiration. Extend that antenna of curiosity and you will surely catch an original thought.

It was an intriguing concept, but light years over my little head. My only concern was how to satisfy my hunger to create. I had become restless using only pencil and paper, and soon adopted a new form of artistic expression. My medium was now tempera paint on cardboard.

To my good fortune, I had an unlimited supply of those most versatile materials. My dad owned and ran a stationary store. Along with selling greeting cards and scented notepaper, it was the only place in town where local businessmen could buy office furniture. Whenever a shipment of file cabinets arrived, I raced over to collect the cardboard containers they came in. Luckily, the store was within walking distance of our house. My neighbors always got a kick from watching that crew cut-headed boy, trotting down the street, dragging a corrugated shipping carton behind him.

I later discovered that cardboard also makes an excellent building material. I immediately set to work constructing cardboard forts and space ships to defend our home against alien invaders. It was a crude form of sculpturing, but I loved it. I was Michelangelo with masking tape and scissors. One Christmas I created a front porch display, featuring the characters from the *Peanuts* comic strip, and left it out overnight to brighten the holidays. I found it the next morning, curled over, bathed in the dew that commonly blankets Bay Area neighborhoods.

One of my more eclectic pieces revealed an unexpected knack for engineering. I formed a face out of a large box. Its features could be manipulated by pulling strings on a control panel. Pull on one and it winked at you. Pull another and an eyebrow went up. Both ears flapped back and forth from a single tug. Think of it as early animatronics, minus the "tronics."

Outside of my immediate family, practically no one else appreciated my cleverness. If I was going to become the next Walt Disney, I had to start focusing on entertaining people. I found that cutting off the top of a file cabinet box and crawling inside made a usable puppet theater. I performed puppet shows for my 4th grade classmates. As I followed a prepared script scotch-taped to the inside, an assistant "outside the box" sat by a record player. Dropping the needle on preselected tracks, the puppets lip-synced to comedy albums, most often to Stan Freberg's hilarious parodies. Puppets with mouths that *didn't* move danced to music. Watching them gyrate to the song "Spunky Onions" became a crowd favorite.

Looking back at my bizarre behavior, my family must have thought I was a few cards short of a full deck, but they tolerated me nonetheless. When I stacked up boxes on our backyard lawn, then crashed into them like a movie stunt double, they withheld judgment. When I followed Popeye's lead by trying to pick up our house after eating a plate of spinach, no one said a word.

I didn't know it at the time, but our uncomplicated life was about to be forever altered. The dawn of the Space Race was now upon us, as people turned their eyes toward the heavens. I remember standing in the street in front of our house, gazing up at the night sky, hoping for a glimpse of Sputnik—the first-ever satellite to orbit the Earth. The whole neighborhood came out to track the mysterious spacecraft. "Look!" someone shouted, pointing up at a moving point of light. We all knew it was probably just a passing airplane. But that didn't dampen our excitement that somewhere up there, history was being made.

Not long after, the promise of modern science would reveal its dark side. Learning that Soviet Russia had acquired a nuclear weapon had the whole nation on edge. A local housing development promoted fallout shelters as a standard feature, which explained why I saw so many rooftop air vents sticking up out of people's front lawns.

But despite the atom bomb tests and threats of foreign aggression, Cold War fears didn't worry us kids. Something wonderful was about to happen. A listing in TV Guide introduced a new program titled *Disneyland*. We watch the first episode. The moment I saw Tinker Bell open the show, I knew everything was going to be alright. She sprinkled her pixie dust to announce that a world of enchantment was coming soon! I had seen Walt's films in theaters, watched his brilliance on TV and read his books. Now, a land named in his honor was being built that I could walk around in. It promised adventures that every mid-century boy dreamed of: exploring spooky island caves, navigating hazardous jungle rivers, blasting into outer space in moon rockets— not to mention flying over Big Ben in a pirate ship with Peter Pan!

One year later, Disneyland opened its gates to the public. I couldn't wait to see it for myself. Only one thing stood in the way: the park was 400 miles down the road in Anaheim. The likelihood of our family traveling there anytime soon didn't look promising.

Then, a *truly* magical thing happened—the kind of magic that not even Walt Disney could have conjured up. My dad had won first place in a sales contest from the Parker Pen Company. The grand prize was an all-expense-paid family vacation to either Las Vegas or Disneyland. Needless to say, the choice was made even before we heard the details.

We instructed the milkman to postpone his deliveries. The newspaper boy was told to bypass our house. We supplied our neighbors with plenty of cat food. And with our bags packed, we drove to the nearest train station.

Next stop: the land of dreams!

1957. 6-year-old Bruce leans on the Main Street Tobacco Shop Indian, only steps away from the Magic Shop.

Chapter 2

All Roads Lead to Anaheim

"Second star to the right, and straight on till morning."
—Peter Pan

The year was 1957. My family and I boarded a train in Oakland, California, bound for Fullerton, and a railroad station near Disneyland. It was an all-day trip, and my parents had their hands full keeping their excited children entertained. For most of the trip we were confined to our assigned seats. My brothers and I played card games to pass the time. But I was a fidgety 6-year-old, and incapable of sitting still for any length of time. I noticed people coming and going through the back door of our passenger car. Naturally curious about everything, I had to see what was on the other side. So when no one was looking, I struck out on my own to investigate.

The process of moving from car to car was straight forward: push on the exit door, then pull on the next car's door to enter it. Forcing the first door open was easy. Tugging on the second one presented a problem: I wasn't strong enough to do it. I was hopelessly stuck between two moving train cars. The swaying motion and the *clickety-clack* on the tracks below frightened me. I began to whimper. Finally, a gentleman on his way to the club car led me back to my seat. My frantic mom was relieved to see me, but made it abundantly clear that I was to stay put. Under the circumstances, I did the only thing I could: I sat quietly, watched the California scenery go by, and at the first opportunity, tried escaping to the next car again.

Eight hours later we arrived in Orange County, where a station wagon waited to take us to the Tops Motel. My first time staying in a strange place was an experience in itself. To begin with, the whole family shared one room. The bathroom towels smelled like they had been laundered in Lysol. But the oddest part was watching the in-room television set. You dropped a quarter into a slot for one hour of viewing time. We tuned in to the *Disneyland* TV show, and watched the theme park on the screen that was only blocks away down Harbor Blvd. After the hour was up, the TV shut itself off, just as *Circus Boy* was coming on.

Before starting our first day at Disneyland, my brothers and I put on our matching red cowboy hats. This was my mom's solution to locating us should we get separated. I often played Cowboy back home, with my Hopalong Cassidy cap gun and holster, so I was all for it. If anyone thought wearing the hats was overkill, my shenanigans on the train more than demonstrated their necessity.

Stepping inside the park, I knew how Stone Age Man felt seeing his first solar eclipse: hard to believe, yet undeniably real. In a word, I was dumbfounded.

Our first stop wasn't actually a "land," per se. It was an avenue of turn-of-the-century curio shops and restaurants: Main Street, U.S.A. Its laid-back atmosphere offered a warm welcome to first-time visitors—inviting and friendly. Period music and horse-drawn streetcars lulled you back to a simpler time. Though my folks were utterly enchanted, my brothers and I saw it only as a launching pad to the magical lands we were anxious to explore. Ragtime pianos and barbershop quartets were fine for grownups, but our sights were set on the central hub—the gateway to fantasy and adventure. We raced down the street, as Mom and Dad watched three red cowboy hats bob up and down toward Sleeping Beauty Castle.

Crossing the drawbridge into Fantasyland, the first order of business was to locate the "dark rides," where small vehicles guide you through recreations of classic Disney films. Snow White and Her Adventures and Mr. Toad's Wild Ride were definitely on our list. But at the very top was Peter Pan's Flight.

Sailing that little pirate ship over the rooftops of London was my multiplane dream come true. Upon landing, a bonus awaited us at the exit: Captain Hook's pirate ship, anchored off the shores of Skull Rock—big as life and accurate in every detail. The one thing missing were the bottles of rum the crew so ferociously swilled in the animated movie. Chicken of the Sea tuna sandwiches and sodas were the only items available for consumption.

I did a lot more flying that first day. I rode on the back of a flying elephant and floated high above the world in a bucket in the sky. The Rocket to the Moon ride didn't actually leave the ground, only simulated the sensation of being airborne. But I did have my picture taken with a man who had been to space. The clear plastic sphere surrounding his head proved he was the real deal. No one could possibly survive a moonwalk without one.

Whether in the air or on the ground, I loved every ride I went on—except maybe the Mad Tea Party teacups, which spins you around to the brink of nausea. It's interesting, though, how the least complex attractions were the ones I liked the best. The log forts and tree houses on Tom Sawyer Island were simple wooden structures, built on compacted earth, yet I spent more time there than anywhere else. And why not? That was a universe I could understand. The world beyond its shores had nothing like it to offer. I wondered: Why can't real life be more like Disneyland?

Six years passed before I returned to Disneyland. It was 1963, and many new and more exciting attractions had been added—the Matterhorn Bobsleds, the Monorail, and the Submarine Voyage among them. Gone were the Junior Autopia cars and Frontierland stagecoaches, but I didn't miss them. I was now 12 years old, and far too advanced for those kiddie rides. I was halfway to manhood, after all.

My creative energy had also taken off in a new direction. The visual arts that had been my preferred form of artistic expression shifted to music. The sound of West Coast Jazz had been filling our house for as long as I could remember. I grew up listening to artists like Dave

Brubeck, Stan Getz, Gerry Mulligan, and Vince Guaraldi. My brothers were now playing musical instruments. Bob was taking piano lessons, and Phil was already in the Novato High School band. It wasn't long before they formed their own Jazz quartet. Not wanting to be left out, I decided to follow Mouseketeer Cubby O'Brian's example. I began taking drum lessons, on a secondhand kit my dad picked up from a pawn shop.

Our newfound passion for music also affected how we experienced Disneyland. Of course, we rode the rides, ate Mickey Mouse pancakes, and shook hands with the walk-around characters. But we spent considerably more time at the Carnation Plaza Gardens stage, tapping our toes to the sound of the Elliot Brothers swing band. We bought their *Date Nite at Disneyland* record album and got every player to sign it.

Two years and dozens of drum lessons later, I was ready to enter the musical family circle. My brothers decided that I was now good enough to play with them. We formed a *rock* band, which was odd, because we had always considered Rock 'n' Roll an inferior genre. Jazz was in our blood, and we listened to nothing else. But the emergence of the Beatles changed our perception of pop music. We willingly abandoned our Jazz roots to adopt a style of music we previously disdained.

We named our new band The Beat-ables, and began performing in and around the San Francisco Bay Area. We played and sang at school dances, private parties, boat ramp openings, any gig we could get. The more we played, the better we got, until we gained a reputation for the quality of our sound. This was especially rewarding for me. I had just started high school, and was making more money each week playing drums than my buddies at their jobs flipping burgers. Not bad for a 14-year-old!

1967. The author (right) with his older brothers Bob (left) and Phil, in their rock band The Beat-ables.

Wanting to extend my musical reach, I tried my hand at songwriting. I taught myself to play piano and began composing rock tunes for our band to play. Meanwhile, oldest brother Phil had found work as an audio engineer at a major San Francisco recording studio. He caught on fast, and quickly became a master of his craft. But more importantly, he had the keys to the studio! The brothers were ready to delve into recording, and occupied the studio after business hours. The owners did not object, so long as our recording time didn't conflict with their paying clientele. Many weekends were spent recording in all-night sessions. At dawn we would emerge, exhausted, yet never more gratified.

San Francisco was now the epicenter of the late '60s rock music explosion. Recording artists migrated to the Bay Area in search of the "San Francisco sound." Bands like Santana, Sly and the Family Stone, and the Grateful Dead all recorded in the same studios my brothers and I did. Though you wouldn't describe us as Flower Children, we tried our best to keep in step with that hippie culture. Wearing our flashy Nehru jackets, we opened for big-name bands in ever larger venues, including San Francisco's Fillmore Auditorium.

As time passed, so did the counterculture movement. The hippies who had flocked to the city took their Frisbees and went home. I was now looking toward college, in search of establishing a more stable career. Architecture seemed like the way to go. I could draw and design as I always liked to do, and be well paid for it. I attended a reputable San Francisco college of engi-neering and went at it full force. That was before learning that once certified as a Designer, I faced a 15-year apprenticeship before reaching my ultimate goal. I didn't want to wait that long. I stuck it out for one year, then quit, with no master plan for the future.

It was a bold move, but my timing couldn't have been worse. The Viet Nam War was still raging. I didn't fully understand what it was all about. I had led a sheltered life, growing up in the most secure and prosperous time in American history. Suddenly, I was ripe for the pickin' by the military draft board. President Nixon had enacted the lottery system for recruiting 19-year-olds. Just my luck, I was the right age, and my number was up next. No big deal, I thought. I would serve my 18 months, then resume college after I got out. But as fate would have it, I flunked my Army physical, disqualifying me for military service. After all my preparations, they didn't want me! That rejection would send me down an entirely new path toward destinations unknown. I needed to reassess my life.

But first . . . Disneyland!

Visiting that wellspring of inspiration was just what I needed. The Pirates of the Caribbean and Haunted Mansion rides had recently opened. A new Disney inno-vation called Audio-Animatronics introduced the world to realistic 3-dimensional animation. I had seen this tech-nology used before in Adventureland's Enchanted Tiki Room, but this was far grander—stunningly visual and much more theatrical.

I wanted to know how it all worked. I rode these amazing rides over and over to study the character's movements. After all, no one was there to tell me not to. Cruising around Disneyland all by myself was a liberating experience. I could wander about as I pleased with no set agenda. I felt more connected with Walt's creation than ever before.

I only stayed one day. Then, like Moses wandering in the wilderness, I roamed the deserts of the American Southwest, until my head was purged of all clutter. Taking in the sights from my '68 Volkswagen beetle, I endured 115-degree heat in the daytime, slept under a billion stars at night, nearly capsized in a flash flood, and kneeled down to the majesty of the Grand Canyon. It was like a religious experience without the theological constraints. Throughout my travels, those old mantras kept repeating in my ear: Follow your dreams! Risk it all! Walt did, so why shouldn't you?

I returned home with a whole new outlook. My pathway was clear: I would resume the musical journey I had started. I enrolled in San Francisco's Music and Arts Institute, where I studied all the things a self-taught musician should know, but never learned.

I rejoined my brothers to form a new band, cleverly named The Edwards Brothers. We took our 3-piece group on the road, playing the big Lake Tahoe casinos and nightclubs up and down the West Coast. In search of bigger and better gigs, we expanded our little trio into a 9-piece horn band. After a time, Phil bowed out. Why go gallivanting around the country with his brothers when he could stay put, living comfortably as a recording engineer? Bob and I continued on as a duo for a while, until tiring of driving those long winter highways through the Pacific Northwest. But for me, the music played on.

It freed me up to pursue more artistic prospects. I headed south to Los Angeles, where the climate was more forgiving and work for musicians more plentiful.

My studio recordings became my calling card. Most of the struggling musicians I met were astounded that I had been inside a professional studio, much less *recorded* in one. I had no idea what a rare gift I had been given. Those tapes opened doors I wouldn't have entered otherwise. I freelanced as a studio musician and joined several local LA rock bands. Disco soon came to dominate contemporary music, and I drummed with bands that played that style. With great humility, I wore my polyester jumpsuits without objection.

My songwriting skills had improved dramatically—so much so that I was invited to pitch tunes to major Hollywood publishing houses, including Chappell Music, whose composers included Rodgers and Hammerstein. I was even offered a publishing deal by Frank Sinatra's manager. But after thorough review and consideration, I was told that my material showed no commercial potential.

Work for Disco bands became increasingly hard to find. Club owners discovered that disc jockeys provided a cheaper alternative to paying a group of musicians. I moved to Orange County in hopes of picking up some lounge work, but that, too, went nowhere. I picked up one-nighters here and there, but not enough to live on.

I was now firmly rooted in Southern California with no livelihood to speak of. Seven years had passed since my awakening in the desert, and nothing worked out like

I had planned. What I didn't know at the time was that Walt Disney was looking over my shoulder. For as long as I could remember, his genius had been my primary source of inspiration. The road I'd been traveling on had brought me to Anaheim, and Disneyland was right in my backyard. Once again, the Happiest Place on Earth would steer me in a surprising new direction.

Chapter 3

Summer of '77

"Do you want an adventure now, or would you
like to have your tea first?"

—Peter Pan

"I like people," I assured my job interviewer. I had been told that making that statement would almost certainly guarantee me a position at Disneyland. I needed a job. That was true. But I had ulterior motives for wanting to work there. All my life I had observed the park as an outsider. This was a chance to look behind closed doors, to examine the machinery and see what made it tick. The only thing standing in my way was my lackluster resume: two years of college, a small-time musician, and practically nothing in the way of working-class experience.

Despite my mediocre qualifications, I was confident things would work out. Like so many others at that time, I was basking in the positive glow that now swept over the country. A charismatic leader was in the White House, the Space Shuttle had completed its first test flight, and a little movie titled *Star Wars* introduced the world to the Force. Baby Boomers who had endured the Viet Nam War and the Watergate hearings welcomed this new age of optimism.

As for me, I was ready for whatever challenges might lay ahead as a Disneyland employee. Besides, how hard could the work be? From what I heard, working at The Happiest Place on Earth was like being on a 40-hour-week vacation.

A short time later I received a letter from Disneyland Recruitment. To my utter amazement, they hired me!

Strangely, this was the first *real* job I'd ever had. Up till now I made my living through either freelancing or self-employment. I had been making music since I was 14, and had never drawn a regular paycheck. At the ripe old age of 26, I was just now joining the great American workforce.

Accepting the job did not include choosing what I would do, or where in the park I wanted to work. After assessing your job history and capabilities, the recruiters placed you where they felt you were best suited. Having experience in the recording industry, they considered placing me in the Audio Division. But the department heads were looking for sound system designers, with the kind of technical skills I didn't have. It was finally determined that I would make an excellent Merchandise Host, probably because I grew up in the shadow of a retail store.

The idea of ringing a cash register all day long didn't particularly appeal to me. I would be standing behind sales counters, selling trinkets to out-of-towners, all to impress the old folks at home where they had gone on vacation. I would have preferred shouting "All aboard!" as a Disneyland Railroad conductor, or wearing a futuristic outfit while piloting the Monorail. To further fuel my disappointment, I had been assigned to Main Street, the most humdrum piece of real estate in the park. The glowing optimism I had walked in with wasn't shining quite so brightly now. What had I gotten myself into?

Every new hire attended a day-long orientation at Disneyland University. This school was not actually a college campus as the name implies, rather a room in an on-site administration building. There you learned the park's policies and procedures, as well as its history.

Each student received a brochure detailing the "Disney Look" that cast members were required to abide by:

HOST HAIR

"The hair is to be neatly groomed so that it does not extend beyond or cover any part of your ears. Hair must not stick out over your shirt collar. Any extreme hair styling . . . such as that of shaving the head and eyebrows . . . is not permitted. Sideburns should be neatly trimmed and may be permitted to extend to the bottom of the earlobe, following their natural contour. Flares and muttonchops are not permitted."

HOST SHOES

"Hosts in costume are requested to wear plain black leather laced oxford shoes with defined heels and black socks. Earth shoe styles and wedge styles are not a prescribed shoe. Shoes should be polished and in good repair at all times."

Next came a group excursion around Disneyland, where we viewed the behind-the-scenes activities hidden from park guests. We were shown the employee cafeterias, locker room locations, and where and how to check out your costume. A little trivia was thrown in to keep it interesting. Actually, the tour was the best part of my indoctrination, having never before seen the park's inner sanctum.

A cheeseburger-and-fries lunch was provided, courtesy of the Hungry Bear Restaurant in Bear Country. This gave our group members a chance to get better acquainted. Most of them were younger than me—many were students attending Cal State University, Fullerton. I must have looked about their age, because everyone kept asking me what classes I was taking. I met one guy who had landed a position in Operations. This was the department I had hoped to work in. There was great prestige in running those amazing rides, not to mention a heftier paycheck.

Back in the classroom, our training concluded with our group being asked a fundamental question: What is Disneyland's product? A variety of answers came back: Thrilling rides. Entertaining shows. Souvenirs. Though these were all valid responses, each was the wrong one. The correct answer lay at the very core of why Walt built the park in the first place. Our product? *Happiness!*

Day One

The morning sun crept slowly over the spires of Sleeping Beauty Castle. Turn-of-the-century songs, like "After the Ball is Over" and "In the Good Old Summertime," played over the Main Street sound system. The park was virtually empty—something Walt Disney never wanted guests to see. But for workers on the opening shift it was a common sight.

With my hair properly trimmed and my dress shoes all shined up, I walked "on stage" for the first time as a Disneyland cast member. Spotting rookie employees isn't hard to do. An invisible halo of giddiness follows them wherever they go. They seem to walk on air, as if having just been sprinkled with pixie dust. Then it hit me that I had that fairy stuff all over me, too. Those little touches only cast members get to experience gave me goose bumps. Behind the Emporium I heard elephants trumpeting their threats to Jungle Cruise boat passengers. Gunshots rang out as their skippers terrorized robot hippos.

Behind City Hall sat the upstairs entrance to Walt Disney's apartment—his personal retreat from the crowds whenever he visited the park. I begged for a peek inside, but the former private residence was strictly off limits to uninvited guests.

That disappointment didn't phase me one bit. Just being there was reason enough to feel happy. I was an integral part of that fantasy world that so profoundly impacted my childhood. I walked the backstreets and hallways that once lay under Walt's feet. If that didn't give you a special feeling, then this was a Laughin' Place you didn't belong in.

For management purposes, the shops were divided into two distinct departments: Main Street West and Main Street North. The West side was dominated by the Emporium, the largest store on the street. The North comprised most everything else: the Camera Shop, Market House, Tobacco Shop, Candy Palace, and more. I would float between most all of these locations as part of the North side group.

Besides ringing cash registers, my job description included performing other retail-related tasks. My first assignment was to stock store shelves, then replenish them throughout the day. With my trusty hand truck, I ferried cartons from various locations behind Main Street. I stocked the Candy Palace bins with chocolate from an underground refrigerated stockroom. I dodged horse-drawn streetcars delivering pickle barrels and apple cider to the Market House. Besides providing an essential service, it was an efficient way to get familiar with the goods sold at each location.

Then came the day I tossed aside my stockman's uniform to don the traditional Main Street costume. Interacting with park guests was enlightening to say the least. Behind the Candy Palace counter, I watched the parade of plump men and women march toward me, their arms laden with 5-pound fudge trays. In the Market House I doled out cookies of all kinds for people to nibble on. Mornings in the Camera Shop was a "zoo," as guests stampeded across the checkered floor to buy film for their Kodak Instamatic cameras.

Working the Tobacco Shop presented its own unique challenges for non-smokers like me. An enormous rack behind the counter held every kind of cigarette imaginable, from American brands to exotic varieties for our foreign guests. Most of the time I spent fetching single packs on request. A European man asked me for twenty of a certain brand. As I proceeded to bag up twenty individual packs, I heard chuckling. Unbeknownst to me, asking for "twenty," the number of smokes in a pack, was how people asked for them in his home country.

On one wall, an open doorway led to the Magic Shop next door. I would occasionally hear applause coming from inside. Then I'd hear shrieks of terror, followed by laughter. What was going on in there? Was this a shop or a showplace? As it turns out, a little bit of both. Not that guests couldn't be entertained elsewhere on Main Street. Glass blowers demonstrated their talents at the Crystal Arts Shop. Candy makers concocted confectionery delights at the Candy Palace. All well and good. But the interaction between hosts and guests at the Magic Shop was something altogether different.

When things were slow in Tobacco, I'd stand in the doorway and watch the resident magicians perform tricks. The first thing I noticed was their attire. They didn't wear the standard Main Street costumes the rest of us did. They wore white shirts instead of striped ones, and blue blazers instead of vests. There was something different about their manner, too. They were a carefree bunch— like unsupervised children in a public playground.

In my younger days, I hadn't considered performing magic as a creative outlet. Something about it didn't appeal to me. Once I bought a Ball and Vase trick at a local five-and-dime. I performed it for my friends, but when I finished, few wanted to see it again. One time I saw Magician Mark Wilson perform his signature illusion on TV: Levitation—where a lovely assistant floats in mid air with no visual means of support. The spectacle had everyone guessing how he did it. I didn't especially care to know.

But despite my indifference toward big stage illusions, what I saw performed in the Magic Shop intrigued me. It's called *close-up* magic. Manipulating cards and coins right under someone's nose requires a different skill set. Sleight of hand isn't only employed to cheat gamblers in a shell game, it's an art form. I wondered how difficult it would be to learn the technique behind it.

"Got Camels?" I heard a guest behind me say. Running back to the Tobacco Shop counter, I thought to myself, You can do better than this!

After my shift was over, I dashed upstairs to my supervisor's office and asked to be reassigned to the Magic Shop. I argued that it was a much better fit for someone with my background. I pointed out my years of performing music before live audiences. What I didn't know about magic I could learn from the shop magicians. To my way of thinking, if they really cared about our guest's "happiness," they would listen to my appeal. Thankfully, they did.

MAGIC MOMENT
A Men's Room with Character

Wander off from Main Street's main drag and you'll likely come across a sign that reads, *Disneyland Cast Members Only.* This indicates where employees can access the backstage area. Curious guests would love to see what's around that corner, but the view is meant for the eyes of that select group only. The park's designers took great pains to control what guests see, and more importantly, what they don't. The berm surrounding the park prevents visitors from being distracted by the outside world. Concealing the goings-on backstage further maintains the integrity of that experience.

Since I was permitted to enter that private hideaway, I saw all those things that were purposely hidden from the public. I saw human heads poking out the top of Disney character costumes. I saw the drab stucco backside of Space Mountain. Aside from that, it was an ordinary work environment. Delivery trucks came and went. The

rumbling of air conditioners cooled the various buildings. Not all cast members who hung out there wore
costumes. Custodians and general maintenance crews, in
standard work clothes, were seen regularly. Except for the
walk-around characters on their breaks, there really
wasn't anything special to see. But on one occasion, I
viewed something that was truly out of the ordinary.

I had only been on the Disneyland payroll for a week,
and was still wrapped in that cloak of euphoria that
comes with working at the Happiest Place on Earth. My
lunch break was almost over. Before returning to my
duties, I visited a backstage men's room. Again, there was
nothing special about it. Pluto was not on the soap
dispensers. Chip and Dale didn't remind you to wash
your hands before leaving.

I stepped into one of the stalls and latched the door
shut behind me. Then I heard the restroom door open
and the sound of someone else coming in. From under
the stall panel I watched a pair of 18-inch-long leather
shoes walk over to the sink. The cuffs of a pair of blue
flannel trousers were draped over them. Yes, it was that
long-eared friend to Mickey and Donald. Finding him in
any other lavatory would have been odd, but not here.
Where else can you find animated characters attending to
their personal needs. I was a newbie, and not yet
accustomed to the sights cast members see in the course
of a normal day.

Just to qualify, the person with whom I shared that
space wasn't really that endearing Disney character, just
someone in a costume that looked like him. Under those

baggy pants, green hat and four-fingered gloves, he was just like you and me. But that's what the backstage area is for. It's a place where cartoon mice and storybook princesses can turn back into humans for a while. It also serves as a reminder, that whether behind the scenes or under a costume, it's the cast members who make Disneyland function.

For the record, this is not the kind of story one repeats in distinguished company. How people spend their private time is nobody's business. I provide this merely as a heads-up to anyone with ambitions of working at Disneyland: expect the unexpected!

Chapter 4

Little Shop of Magic

"You just think lovely wonderful thoughts."

—Peter Pan

"**C**oat Size?" asked the nice lady behind the Wardrobe Department window. I didn't give her my chest width or arm length. Instead, I stated my name. Over the counter she passed me a blue blazer with *Bruce Edwards* inked across the inside label. A considerate seamstress had altered the garment's sleeve length to match my extra-long arms. Before heading onstage, I glanced into a mirror to be sure my black bow tie was on straight. I was dressed to kill in the official costume of the Main Street Magic Shop!

The light bulbs following the contours of the Main Street buildings had just come on. A light Santa Ana breeze promised a comfortable summer evening ahead. On popped the chaser lights that circled the Magic Shop sign, welcoming me inside as its newest shopkeeper.

This was my first real look at what would become my permanent workspace. It was a small, but comfortable room, though oddly shaped. The angled walls met at the back, acting like a giant funnel to draw people inside. Like the rest of the street, the visual style embraced the charm of a bygone era. You almost expected to see gas flames flickering in the ceiling light fixtures. Breathing in that masculine scent from the Tobacco Shop, I imagined mustached men in a Victorian parlor, holding out their cigars, as they relaxed in plush velvet chairs.

Although Main Street resembled a typical downtown in the 1890s, I doubt that a magic shop would have been among the storefronts. Merchants primarily catered to the basic needs of its local citizens. Still, stage magicians were in their heyday around that time, and the shop offered a taste of why so many flocked to see the likes of Thursten, Dante and The Great Blackstone.

Besides the shop's mystical ambiance, a kind of childlike foolhardiness filled the air. I felt it the moment I looked around me: the yellow rubber chickens, the chattering false teeth, the huge rubber iguana stretched out on top of the cash register. I hadn't been there five minutes before that sense of frivolity overwhelmed me. In the midst of Main Street's quaint respectability, the Magic Shop offered a good time for all, as if to say, Come in and be amazed! Stop by for a laugh!

Stepping behind the counter, I was surrounded by Disneyland history. The display cases had been hand built by the shop's founder, Merv Taylor. He had been designing and constructing magician's stage props in Hollywood since the 1940s. At Walt Disney's request, he set up Merlin's Magic Shop in Fantasyland in time for the park's opening. Located only steps from Sleeping Beauty Castle,

Merlin's projected a medieval theme. Step inside and you'd find spooky owls and suits of armor. The more elegant Main Street shop displayed vaudeville posters, featuring magicians with little red devils whispering in their ears. My favorite one showed a green, pointy-toothed ogre, dunking Harry Houdini into his famous water torture tank.

One other historical note: I doubt that there is a Disneyland fan alive who doesn't know that comedian Steve Martin once worked there. The comic legend had left the park years before I came on board. And though he spent most of his time at Merlin's, his presence in the Main Street shop is felt to this day.

Acquainting myself with the shop's stock-in-trade was next. On the pegboard walls hung dozens of easy-to-learn tricks, like Cups and Balls, the Chinese Bottle, and one where little foam rabbits multiply in your hand. The more professional tricks were kept behind the counter. Due to limited space, we didn't sell large stage illusions. But we did carry a variety of parlor tricks, suitable for performing before smaller audiences. These included classics like the Chinese Linking Rings and the Zombie Ball floating sphere illusion.

Anyone who enjoys playing practical jokes on people found an assortment of simple gags. For the uninitiated, here's a breakdown of our most popular pranks and what they do:

SNAKE CANS: A one-quart tin can labeled *Peanut Brittle*. Unscrew the cap and two fabric-covered springs launch into the air. Load up to 6 snakes in one can for greater impact. Also available in convenient mixed-nut size.

CONDIMENT SQUEEZE BOTTLES: Point this common restaurant table item at your intended target and squeeze. A colored string spews out the tip, creating the effect that you've just soiled your victim with a greasy liquid. Choose between yellow mustard or red ketchup containers.

JOY BUZZERS: A palm-sized, wind-up gadget that shocks anyone you shake hands with. Contrary to popular belief, this devise does not deliver an electric shock, only a physical vibration you're not expecting, thereby the "buzz" in its name.

ELECTRIC SHOCK GAGS: Conversely, this prank uses a battery to inflict a jolt of real electricity. Though technically harmless, the "zap" you feel is really your shattered self-importance. Comes in either book form or as a cigarette lighter. Not recommended for use on people with pacemakers!

Of course, we didn't stock gags that breached Disney's standard of good taste. Noticeably absent were Whoopee Cushions, fake vomit and plastic dog poop. There was, however, one item that illustrates how attitudes have changed since the 1970s. *Black Soap* looked like an ordinary cleansing bar. But wash your hands with it and your skin turns black! Not to worry, though. The ink safely rinses off under running water. It wasn't so much the gag that would offend people today. It was the packaging. It showed a man desperately wiping the blackness off his *face,* as the perpetrator laughs hysterically, shouting, "What a sucker!" Good luck selling that in today's "woke" culture.

We also sold items that had nothing to do with magic or gags. Most notable were the latex masks of famous horror film personalities, like Frankenstein's Monster and the Creature from the Black Lagoon. A line of *Star Wars* characters had recently been added from Don Post Studios—Hollywood's premier mask maker. Checking the hefty price tags on Darth Vader and Chewbacca explained why so many guests came in just to admire them. "Hey, look!" they'd say, "C-3PO!" then leave.

But as strange and wonderful as the Magic Shop was, most guests didn't come in to browse our merchandise. They didn't reach for the fly-in-the-ice cube gag, or the Money Maker magic trick. They headed for the counter to the man in the blue blazer, for a show they couldn't see anywhere else.

In that spotlight stood a group of talented magicians. Foremost among them was Mark Neynaber. No one was more knowledgeable, skillful, or committed to the art form than he was. He could fan a deck of cards with the precision of a Swiss watchmaker. Performing since the age of 5, he had been welcomed into The International Brotherhood of Magicians, and belonged to Hollywood's prestigious Magic Castle. He didn't just impress guests with his ability, he *dazzled* them!

Mark Neynaber: The technical wizard.

Jim Everett and Chuck Lucas were also masters of the magical arts. Like Mark, both were Magic Castle members, which meant that they had earned their magician's stripes. I refer to them jointly, because you rarely saw one without the other. They were like Martin and Lewis, each one a comedic sidekick to the other. Whenever they were around, the shop felt more like a college frat house. To guests they were always courteous and friendly. But when they wished someone a nice day at Disneyland, they were really saying, Let's get this party started!

Chuck Lucas and Jim Everett: Party on!

And finally, the headliner of the show. Ken Neufeld was a Main Street legend long before I arrived. Having already worked there eight years, he was the grand master, the elder statesman. His free-and-easy approach to performing magic stood in stark contrast to Mark's dynamic style. Interestingly, Ken was not a Magic Castle member, nor had he been honored by the magic community. You didn't see any eye-popping illusions in his presentations, and yet, he always seemed to draw the largest crowds.

Ken Neufeld: The grand master.

Initially, Ken and I worked opposite shifts, until I finally got the chance to watch him perform. His patter was hilarious, and I laughed along with everyone else. I later learned that he was merely reciting the instructions that came bundled with each trick, only going off-script in response to his audience's reaction. He proved that it isn't the words you speak, but how you deliver them that wins the day.

I would be remiss if I didn't acknowledge the supporting cast who also made this show a success. Though playing 2nd fiddle to these virtuosos of magic, they were no less essential in keeping the shop humming: Harry Snowden, Jim Turner, Jim Stitt, Irma Quintana, Bob

Gordon, and Christy Sims to name a few.

My introduction to the Main Street Magic Shop was both stimulating and bewildering at the same time. I was seeing it through the eyes of a first-time visitor. The only difference was that I wouldn't be moving on to see other Disneyland attractions. I would be sticking around to see what happens next. For me, the curtain was now about to rise on Act II: learning to perform magic.

On with the show!

So I've Been Told

Lessons From a Cigar Store Indian

It was Chuck Lucas' first day as a Disneyland cast member, and the first time he would enter the Magic Shop as a Main Street Merchandise Host. When starting any new job, it's always a good idea to be on time. The new hire was scheduled to start work at 10:30 in the morning, but that was not what he read on the time sheet. It said to show up at 10.50 (note the decimal point). He didn't know that shifts were assigned in *digital* hours, and interpreted his start time to mean 10:50 instead of 10:30. Consequently, he arrived at his first day on the job 20 minutes late!

Behind the counter stood Ken Neufeld, staring at his wrist watch, shaking his head disapprovingly. That was when Chuck learned that he had misread the work schedule. He hoped to hear some reassuring words, such as, *That's okay. We all do it,* but heard nothing of the kind. Ken showed him around the shop and described the duties he was to perform. Then Ken said, "I have some business to take care of. Be back in a few minutes." This was not exactly the warm welcome Chuck had expected.

A short time later the phone rang. When Chuck answered it, a man on the other end asked to speak to Mr. Lucas. It was his supervisor! Apparently, the "business" Ken was attending to included informing Chuck's boss of his tardiness. To confirm that the latecomer was really there, the man instructed Chuck to go outside and stand next to the Tobacco Shop's cigar store Indian. He would look for him through his 2nd-story office window across the street. "Wave to me," he said, "so I know that it's you."

Chuck did as he was told. He stood beside the wooden statue, staring up at the velvet-draped window and waving. 15 minutes passed and he had yet to see anyone appear. The curtains didn't so much as flutter. Then he heard the sound of laughter trickling out through the Magic Shop door. It turns out that Main Street's entire 2nd floor is just an empty facade. The supervisor who called Chuck was actually Ken, using the Tobacco Shop phone next door.

Red-faced, Chuck returned to the Magic Shop, a victim of a hilarious prank. After recovering from his embarrassment, he learned that this kind of mischief was par for the course in the Magic Shop. Playing gags, whether on park visitors or on each other, was a long-standing tradition. He had just been formally inducted into that quirky club of pranksters.

He should have been angry over the incident. No one likes to look foolish. If standing on that busy sidewalk, searching for a nonexistent supervisor wasn't bad enough, forcing him to wave his arms like a marooned sailor was beyond mean. Yet Chuck harbored no resentment. He laughed at being so easily duped. The only person not smiling was that cigar-toting statue outside. He was rigid. Immovable. Unyielding. Yet his stone-faced silence had something to teach us all: Until we learn to laugh at ourselves, we're no more human than a cigar store Indian.

Miniature model of the Magic Shop interior,
built by Chuck Lucas.

Chapter 5

Do a Trick!

"Oh, the cleverness of me!"

—Peter Pan

Curious as it seems, many who visit Disneyland make the Main Street Magic Shop their first stop, anxious to see what's changed or to learn a new trick. Once inside, the first thing a cast member hears is: "Will you show me some magic?" Back in the day, that request was always directed toward a blue-blazered magician. Anyone donning the traditional Main Street attire was pegged as a stand-in for the real thing. Though I wore one of those signature sports jackets, I had yet to learn any tricks. If asked to perform one, I would point to that day's designated magician and say, "Go ask him."

There were two kinds of magicians in the shop: illusionists, and the ones who demonstrated tricks. Demonstrators generated sales, not unlike those door-to-door peddlers who show you how to operate their vacuum cleaners. It was the illusionists' job to entertain, whether a trick sold or not. This was the esteemed group I wanted to belong to.

At the time my knowledge of magic didn't extend beyond Marshall Brodien's TV Magic Cards. To illustrate just how naive I was, I didn't know the secret behind the Chinese Sticks—a simple trick anyone can do. The props consisted of two traditional-looking magic wands, with a tasseled yellow string protruding from the end of each one. Pulling down on one tassel caused the string on the other wand to go up. You presumed that the strings were somehow linked together, yet the wands were kept far apart, with no visible connection.

As I watched Ken Neufeld perform this trick, I was as confounded as the 5-year-old he was showing it to. I hadn't a clue how ridiculously simple the gimmick was. I'm not an idiot (though this is widely disputed), but I felt like one, unable to solve the riddle of a $2.50 trick.

The Chinese Sticks: Any idiot can do it.

Ken ended his routine by inviting a spectator to pull down on a tassel, whereupon the other string just sat there. "You broke it," he nonchalantly remarked. To show there were no hard feelings, he offered the guest a tin of peanut brittle, from which sprang two snake-like projectiles.

Like all good magicians, Ken would not reveal how the trick is done, so the onlookers turned to me to divulge it. When faced with this dilemma, there are two ways you can respond: 1. Tell them you can do it, but the magician's code won't allow you to say how. Or 2. Admit that you had been stumped by a trick that any simpleton could figure out.

A little girl approached me and asked to see a different trick. This time I gallantly brought out the only one I knew: Ball and Vase. As I proceeded to astound my audience of one, my hands began to tremble—a sure giveaway that you're watching a novice at work. But I made it to the end without making too big a fool of myself.

As with any trick, there is always that moment after the final reveal when time stands still. You either get a round of applause or dead silence. Luckily, this little one was utterly mystified. Her look of astonishment was priceless. She turned to her friends and exclaimed, "Did you see that?" I felt 10-feet tall. But my self-confidence quickly vaporized when she uttered that inevitable follow up: "Do another one!"

If I was going to live up to the title of Magic Shop Magician, I definitely needed to expand my repertoire. I could rise to that level by reading books on Magic. We sold the renowned Tarbell series—a 10-volume collection that disclosed all the secrets you'd ever need to know. I knew

I'd never find the patience for that. Besides, interpreting those instructions is like trying to decipher ancient hieroglyphics. But I was saved from all that tedium by Magician Mark Neynaber, who graciously took me under his wing. Slowly but surely, the mystery of magic was unveiled to me. He gave me advanced instruction on how to execute card tricks with a regular deck. The other shop magicians were my teachers as well, though they didn't know it. Each of them had his own style and patter that I ruthlessly plundered.

As any magician will tell you, mastering this craft takes practice. So, that's just what I did. Before long I had mastered every trick in the shop. Along the way I discovered that the simplest ones could be the most entertaining when presented in a novel way. The variations were endless. This was the kind of creative challenge I liked: to put a fresh spin on centuries-old routines.

But why go to all that trouble? Why not just do these tricks the same way they've always been done? I guess it's because people deserve variety. Imagine going into a restaurant to find only one item on the menu. It may be a sumptuous dish, but until you provide alternatives, people will never know what they're missing. Offering something original adds flavor to a chronically bland world.

Besides, if it made my audience happier, that was all that mattered. On rare occasion, magicians came on board who showed little concern for our guests' well-being. They were only there to show off. After a trick, they'd display that cocky, I-know-the-secret-and-you-don't attitude. You could always tell, because they'd end each trick wearing a smirk instead of a smile.

Their talent for stealing the spotlight also made things difficult for their co-workers. On busy nights, the rule was: No demonstrating the final hour before closing. The shop was simply too overrun with shoppers. But while the rest of us scrambled to ring up sales, these hotshots would be off doing magic tricks. Fortunately, their kind didn't stay too long. Put them on cookie duty in the Market House for a week and they'd be gone before you knew it.

You didn't have to be a great magician to show guests a good time. Many of the other Main Street hosts who worked in Magic were hesitant about performing. But after showing them some simple tricks, all those inhibitions melted away. There's an exhilaration you feel when standing before an audience—albeit a small one—and they were keen to give it a try. As beginners they offered no excuses for their inexperience. They gave it their best shot, and if any messed up, we applauded them just the same.

But after a while, many chose to return to their prior locations. Their withdrawal was mostly because they couldn't tolerate some of our younger guests. Most kids came into the shop wanting you to amaze them. If you succeeded, you were commended. "Well done!" But others were there for the sole purpose of lousing up your presentation.

Handling malicious children was all part of the job. These troublemakers were pretty easy to spot. Instead of asking politely to see some magic, they'd charge toward the counter and demand, "Do a trick!" The minute you started, they'd insult you by saying something like, "Oh, that lame old trick!"

Then there were the ones hell-bent on exposing your sleight-of-hand moves. They'd pry open your fingers to show what you had hidden in your hand. They'd hoist themselves up onto the counter, then announce to the room where you had stashed a vanished object. Over time you learned to anticipate these interruptions. Keeping those little hooligans at arms length helped protect the integrity of your performance.

For the severely disruptive ones, I applied my own brand of revenge. I'd fan a deck of cards and ask the offensive child to choose one. After returning it to the deck, I attempted to locate it, only to produce the wrong card. Proud of my accomplishment, I placed it face down on the counter. After a round of hurtful laughter, I'd turn it face *up*, revealing that I had indeed found his card. After watching the little brute wipe the egg off his face, I'd invite him to examine what was a standard deck of cards.

I shouldn't be the one to criticize bad behavior. I once came close to ruining the act of world-famous Magician Blackstone, Jr. He had brought his road show to the Orange County Performing Arts Center, and I was in the audience. During intermission, I went to the upstairs balcony. The center had only recently opened, and I wanted to explore this magnificent new showplace. A sign on the door read *Balcony Closed,* but I went inside anyway.

The view of the hall from that height was stunning.

Leaning over for a better look, I discovered two thin wires taped to the railing that led down toward the stage. Blackstone's second act would include floating a glowing orb over the heads of the audience—an illusion that depended on those wires being there. Just like in a cartoon, I felt those devil horns growing out of my scalp. I was faced with two options: leave the wires alone, or peal them away and destroy Blackstone's grand finale. The wicked side of me said pull them off. The magician in me said to leave them be. Having personally been a victim of that kind of sabotage, I didn't have the heart to bungle his trick. Blackstone, Jr. went on to finish his show to thunderous applause!

Turn-of-the-century magicians didn't worry too much about secrets leaking out. Those in the profession kept a tight lid on who knew them and who didn't. But a century later, with the explosion of the internet, anyone with a connected device can learn those secrets. Magic Shop guests with mobile phones will know how the trick is done before you're finished doing it.

In the late 70s that wasn't a problem. The World Wide Web was something less than worldly. Those who owned computers bought them at their local Radio Shack stores, then "dialed up" their internet connections. For us computer illiterates, mention a search *engine* and we pictured a red Corvette, speeding down Route 66. Playing Ms. PAC Man at Shakey's Pizza Parlor was the closest we got to a CPU.

Regardless, the old rule still applied. Revealing the secret was a major no-no. There were times, however, when I felt justified in giving secrets away—to children, mostly. I often saw broader smiles after showing kids how to do a trick, than I saw when they watched me perform it. Besides, how could I know I wasn't inspiring a budding young magician?

Some believe that you can't enjoy magic when you know how the tricks are done. That's not entirely true. I have seen magicians perform ordinary tricks and enjoyed them immensely. Mark Neynaber encouraged me to see one in particular: Harry Anderson. This was before he gained fame in the TV sitcom *Night Court*. The illusions he performed were nothing spectacular, but his routine was hysterical. He had cleverly merged the bravado of stage magic with stand-up comedy. I particularly liked how he performed the Chinese Linking Rings with metal coat hangers. Knowing those secrets did not spoil my evening in the least. It was Harry's comedy-infused pre-sentation that won me over.

When someone asks a magician, How'd you do that trick? there's a tried-and-true method of sidestepping the answer. It's one that surely hearkens back to the days of Houdini. You simply offer that tongue-in-cheek reply: "Very well, thank you." Heaven knows I used it often in the Magic Shop.

But whether I revealed a trick's secret or not was really beside the point. People come to Disneyland from all corners of the globe, from different cultural and social backgrounds. For some it might be the only time they ever step foot in the park. A family may have had to scrape together the price of admission. I like to think that in offering some insight into the world of magic, I've provided that extra measure of happiness they've earned. After all, that's why we were there. And that's no secret!

Pick a card! Ken Neufeld and a ventriloquist puppet perform a card trick. Guess which one is the dummy.

MAGIC MOMENT
That Other Castle

"You ought to audition," said Mark. What my mentor was suggesting was that I join Hollywood's famed Magic Castle. It's a private club for magicians and fans of the magical arts, where you go to eat, drink and be entertained by today's premier illusionists. I had heard of it, of course. What I didn't know was that to gain membership, you had to perform before a panel of master magicians, who then judge your worthiness to belong to that elite organization. Mark felt that I was up to the task.

I wasn't so sure. I only knew the tricks we sold in the shop. How could I possibly win over those seasoned professionals? There were thousands much more proficient at sleight-of-hand magic than me. But Mark assured me that wouldn't be a problem. The judges focus less on your aptitude, and more on the originality of your presentation. "Perform any tricks you like," Mark said.

"Just be sure you execute them in some new way." I decided to go for it.

The night of my audition, I arrived early at that Hollywood hillside manor. I went inside to find a darkened library, straight out of an Agatha Christie novel—stately, yet mysterious. Appropriately, a sliding bookcase revealed the gateway to a world of vintage bars, plush showrooms and a grand mahogany staircase. Some like to compare its interior to Disneyland's Haunted Mansion, which actually did inspire its initial design. I would describe it as hauntingly elegant. But whatever your impression, there is no escaping its spooky ambiance. The eyes in a painted portrait follow you as you walk past it. A chilling seance may be going on in the next room. But fear not. You scarcely hear a door creak. There is no dust on the antiques nor cobwebs in the door frames. If that was a ghost you just bumped into, it was surely a friendly one.

Then I turned around to see Harry Houdini looking down at me from an oil painting. His cold stare reminded me why I had come there. The night had only just begun, and I was starting to feel a bit apprehensive.

After being ushered into a private room, in walked the magic maestros. I recognized one of them from a book we sold in the shop. They introduced themselves, then we all sat down at a round table. I immediately launched into my prepared routine.

It went something like this:

"When I first began performing magic," I said, "I started out small." I laid a pack of *miniature* playing cards on the table. (My attempt at a comedic beginning didn't exactly light up the room.) I continued: "But card tricks weren't the only kind of magic that interested me." Opening the box, there were no cards inside. I pulled 3 small ropes out of it, and proceeded to do an abbreviated version of the Professor's Nightmare rope trick. "Then I got a little bolder." I next produced a regular-sized deck. Again, no cards. I dumped out a set of 3-inch metal rings and performed what I called the Pigmy Linking Rings.

As I was about to bring out one final card deck, they stopped me. "That's enough," said one of the magicians.

"You're in, kid," said another—or something to that effect.

As they rose up from the table, I said, "Don't you want to see my big finish?" then brought out a pack of *jumbo*-sized playing cards. Surprisingly, that actually generated a bit of mild laughter.

And with that, I was welcomed into that exclusive society of magicians!

Some of the perks that came with membership included free admission to the Castle, and unlimited access to its extensive library on magic. Being allowed to enter that nightspot whenever I liked proved to be the most useful benefit. Though a members-only club, anyone could get in with a guest pass, issued by an active member. This allowed family and friends to attend on their own. The catch was that they had to pay an admission fee, as well as dine at the Castle's restaurant. Members were not bound by that requirement, making it more cost effective if I brought people there as my guests.

News of my membership quickly circulated around

Disneyland. It seemed like everyone I knew wanted to visit the Castle. They would each ask me for a guest pass, which I happily provided. But whenever an attractive young lady asked me for one, I instead offered to escort her there personally. Of course, my generosity didn't fool them for a minute. It was my crafty way to spend a night out with a girl on my arm, and they all knew it.

We would begin our evening in my favorite cocktail lounge, where Irma the Ghost played the piano. From an empty piano bench, the invisible lady played tunes on request. You listened to her play, while watching the piano keys rise and fall by themselves.

To further impress my date, I would perform some hocus-pocus of my own, on one of the dozens of felt-covered tables scattered around the club. One night I brought out a deck of playing cards and began a card trick. In an instant, I found myself the center of attention. Surrounding me were other Castle guests, watching me, as if I was a paid performer. Before I knew it, a lady sat down next to me. This one, as they say, had had a few too many. My staple of card tricks failed to impress her. So, I fell back on my "revenge" trick—the one where I pretend to louse up my own routine. She picked a card from the deck, returned it, whereupon I failed to find the one she had selected. This was the exact same deception I used on 10-year-olds in the Magic Shop. Then I revealed the correct card. Presto! My standing audience applauded. Not so the inebriated spectator sitting beside me.

I visited the Magic Castle often during my years at Disneyland. Over time, those visits became less frequent.

But having the distinction of being affiliated with that organization was a great honor. Oftentimes a Magic Shop guest would call on me to perform a trick, then ask, "Have you been to the Magic Castle?" I proudly answered, "I'm a member!"

Chapter 6

Caution: Children at Play

*"I sometimes think that children are more trouble
than they are worth."*

—Wendy

D eny it if you will, but there isn't one of us who
wouldn't like to live forever young. We all wish we
could revisit those playful hours we enjoyed before
growing into responsible adults. Those of us working in
the Magic Shop were given the chance to live out that
fantasy—to recapture our mischievous youth. I'm talking
about the thrill of playing jokes on perfect strangers. Part
of our job was demonstrating the products we sold, and
we obligingly showed guests how to execute pranks with
utmost effectiveness. Make no mistake. The shop was not
there to promote juvenile misconduct. It was a reputable
retail establishment, and we respected that. But, c'mon!
Where else can you embarrass people all day long and get
paid for it?

Elsewhere on Main Street, that kind of monkey
business was not tolerated. Sprinkling hot peppers on
someone's Market House cookie was strictly forbidden.

Confectioners at the Candy Palace were prohibited from adding garlic to their English Toffee. But squirting mustard on a guest was perfectly permissible in the Magic Shop, so long as it was *fake* mustard.

Humiliating people may seem like a mean thing to do. But when you think about it, that very behavior lies at the root of what we now call *schadenfreude:* deriving pleasure from the anguish of others. Not that this is anything new. During the college prank craze of the 1920s, a favorite gag was filling paper bags with water, then dropping them out of hotel windows onto unsuspecting pedestrians below. Dousing a chubby lady, or a man in a custom-tailored suit, made it that much more fun. In those days, playing pranks was considered a young man's rite of passage.

Done properly, pulling off a good gag doesn't have to irritate people. It just requires a little finesse. Walking up to a total stranger and blatantly squirting him with pretend mustard lacks style. You don't want to completely demean your victim, just enough to make him laugh at himself. Timing is everything. Hesitating before aiming your squirt bottle doesn't work if your target already suspects what you're doing. By the same token, doing it prematurely spoils the element of surprise.

For best results, gags should only be attempted following some preliminary action. If someone is chomping down popcorn while you're performing a trick, you pause your routine and say, "Want some mustard on that?" then proceed to squirt them with the phony sauce. Ken Neufeld had the right idea: Whenever he was asked to reveal a trick's secret, he humbly replied, "Sorry, I can't. But you can read all about it in *here!*" then plop down an electric-shock book.

Too many make the mistake of initiating a joke out of revenge. Using a water-squirting gag on people, just because they didn't like your magic trick, doesn't start them laughing. It only makes them angry. Another error is forcing a gag without the proper setup. Holding out a peanut brittle snake can and saying, "Want some?" is a gross misuse of a classic prank. They will see what you're up to and back away, leaving *you* the one looking foolish.

A greatly underappreciated gag is the Dollar Snatcher. It's basically a thin piece of thread, wound around a spring-loaded spool. Extend the thread and tape it to the back of a dollar bill, then lay it somewhere where your intended victim will find it. As he reaches for it, releasing the spring causes the bill to leap back into your hand. I used to attach it to a scrap of sales receipt paper. After completing a purchase, I'd lay it on the counter, then remind the guest, "Don't forget your receipt." As he starts to grab it, zip! That was my wacky way of saying, Have a nice day!

Park guests were not always the target of Magic Shop pranks. Co-workers were just as vulnerable. Chuck Lucas observed that one of the shopgirls habitually kicked her shoes off while standing behind the counter, and decided to have some fun at her expense. While she wasn't looking, he stuffed her shoes into a Disneyland shopping bag, then told her, "A woman left this behind. I just saw her walk into Lost and Found. Take it over there, will you?" The poor girl searched the floor for her shoes, which of course, were no longer there. "Quickly," urged Chuck, "before she leaves!" Lost and Found was only a short distance across the street, so she rushed over in her stocking feet. Stepping inside, the room was empty, except for a kindly cast member. Inspecting the contents of the bag, she discovered she'd been had.

Veteran pranksters were also fair game for these antics. One evening after closing, the night crew stuffed a spring-loaded gag snake into the main register's cash drawer, knowing that Ken Neufeld was scheduled to open the shop the next morning. "But why stop there?" someone asked. "If he jumps a foot off the ground with one snake, he'll hit the ceiling with *ten!*" As predicted, Ken entered the shop alone with the day's cash fund, unaware of the comical explosion that awaited him. Though no one was there to witness the event, a Main Street supervisor reported hearing a scream coming from inside the Magic Shop.

But as much as we enjoyed playing jokes on others, sometimes the joke was on us! The gags we sold were not exactly high-quality products. Invisible Ink, for example, is supposed to fade out after squirting it on someone. One time a guest bought a tube from us and tried it out. As you've already guessed, the ink on the victim's garment only partially dissolved. The item was summarily removed and never ordered again.

The Haunted Mansion Secret Panel Chest was a 6 x 4-inch wooden box that contained hidden compartments. Slide the panels open in the right order to see what's inside. Upon opening one of them, something was found hiding that didn't belong there: Japanese beetles. Either the product had been made from infested lumber, or the little pests lunched on the tasty boxes while in warehouse storage.

The greatest embarrassment by far came from selling our novelty handcuffs. These were solid metal shackles that required a key to unlocked them. The gag was to clap them on someone, then watch your victim squirm when he hears that you've lost the key. Selling a device that police used to arrest criminals, at the Happiest Place on Earth, always bothered me. Then came disturbing news that a woman in Florida had been assaulted while bound in a pair of our handcuffs. I cannot confirm that this actually happened. All I know is that our remaining stock of that item was immediately impounded.

As much fun as all this sounds, too much of a good thing can lead to boredom. Constantly having to amuse guests has its limits. So on slow mornings, with not much to do, we entertained each other. An example of this involved the little toy mice we sold. The furry, 2-inch-tall rodents sat on their haunches, nibbling on a kernel of corn. The gag was to hide one in a coat closet or on a cupboard shelf. Anyone opening the door would mistake it for the real thing and scream at the sight of it.

These cute, cuddly creatures were just begging to be mistreated. A trend emerged when someone began adorning them with miniature accessories. A pirate hat and a patch over one eye became "Pi-*rat.*" A mouse wearing a red cape was named "Little *Rat* Riding Hood." You get the idea.

From left: Rocky *Rat*-ciano, Abe-*rat*-ham Lincoln, Pi-*rat*, and Elvis *Mouse*-ly.

(Simulated image. Not the fa-*mouse* originals.)

Another kind of altered mouse was incorporated into a magic trick. On each countertop lay a demo pad—a thin, felt-covered board on which to demonstrate tricks. Under one was a dissected toy mouse, laying flat on the counter, as if squished under a car tire. At the end of your Cups and Balls routine, you would secretly "load" an undoctored mouse under the cup. Lifting it up showed your audience the surprise hiding inside. Eek! Then you vanished the mouse, while at the same time slamming your hand down on the pad. Turning it over revealed the rodent's flattened remains underneath it! Ugh!

Stars of Magic was a book we sold that featured photos of the creme-de-la-creme of close-up magicians. These images, along with step-by-step instructions, showed how each accomplished his signature illusion. It was discovered that with a little imagination and a pencil eraser, the photos on the glossy pages could easily be altered. Dai Vernon's fanned deck of cards became a butler's tray, from which Slydini's vanishing coins, now Chiclets, were served. Appropriate captions were added to augment the humor.

This "special edition" was prudently hidden under the counter where no one could find it—and for good reason. Some years earlier, a copy of that same book had been similarly modified. For convenience it was kept on display behind the counter, should an inspired magician want to further embellish it. One afternoon, all those who were aware of the book's uniqueness were on their breaks. As fate would have it, the cast member who filled in for them sold it to a guest. Obviously, the purchaser did not bother flipping through the pages before buying it. No attempt was ever made to return the book. Perhaps it was never read, or maybe the owner recognized it as a rare Disneyland collectible. Whatever the reason, the whereabouts of that irreplaceable volume remains a mystery.

Hands-down, my favorite abuse of store merchandise was also the most twisted. A Disneyland buyer purchased a line of plaster figurines of famous horror film icons. Standing about 10 inches tall, they included Dracula, Frankenstein's Monster and The Mummy. Upon closer examination, we observed that the Wolfman statue was posed in a very distinctive way. His bent knees and lowered bottom suggested an action that only a juvenile mind would interpret. It wasn't long before someone procured some Tootsie Rolls from the Candy Palace. The little brown candies were unwrapped and placed under the figure's behind. A roll of cash register receipt tape substituted for toilet tissue, all to support the legend, that while werewolves were murderous creatures of the night, they were also half human.

Why is this werewolf smiling?

Fittingly, we acknowledged the classic character's roots in European folklore by naming it. One of the magicians spoke fluent German, and dubbed our little masterpiece, "Der Volfman Fahrt." Literal translation: the Wolfman takes a . . . trip!

Strangely, we didn't attempt to hide the repulsive figurine. We placed him on a shelf for all to enjoy. But we soon realized that our work of art had crossed the line into the realm of bad taste. We removed the defecating monster from public view, and hid him in a dark corner where he could be safely appreciated. There he sat (or squatted, to be more precise) for years afterward.

If all this sounds like the conduct of naughty little children who should know better, you'd be right. Pulling pranks and defacing property is kids stuff. Grownups have no business exhibiting such immature behavior. We all age, and as we do, we leave that childhood mischief-making behind. But to all those who believe that we're only young *once*, I beg to differ.

MAGIC MOMENT
Along Came a Spider

Each of the two Disneyland magic shops displayed its own unique features. Inside Merlin's Magic in Fantasyland stood a two-foot tall model of the witch from Disney's *Snow White and the Seven Dwarfs*. The black-robed villain spoke to you through the iron bars of a prison cell. She promised that if you set her free, you would be rewarded by learning how to turn water into gasoline. What made this amusing was that the country was in the midst of a gas shortage. President Carter had levied embargoes on the Middle-eastern oil producers, which limited gasoline production in the U.S. Shortages created long lines of cars at gas stations. Political commentary of this kind was rarely expressed inside Disneyland. Remember, you visited that happy place to escape those troubles simmering outside the berm.

Like Merlin's, the Main Street Magic Shop had its own novelty features. Early on I discovered a length of string running along the edge of a shelf behind the counter, having no clue why it was there. But I quickly surmised its purpose, when noticing a 4-inch rubber spider on the ceiling across the room, tied to the other end. Manipulating the cord lowered the spider. In turn, guests standing beneath it felt an unexpected visitor drop down on their heads.

The set up is fairly simple: Install a series of 1/4-inch screw eyes along the path you want the string to take. Thread the string through each opening. Tie your spider to one end of the string, and a handle of some kind to the other. A key ring works well. That's it!

Basic rubber spider gag setup.

Spiders were rigged to terrorize guests in several locations. Of the two used most often, one hung above the book rack by the front door, the other in the back corner above the pegboard displays. Dropping a spider effectively required some degree of skill. You had to take into account your intended victim's position relative to that of the spider. With a little practice, you could land it squarely on someone's head. Hitting a guest's shoulder was missing the bullseye, yet was still acceptable. Precise timing was crucial. Lower a spider too slowly and your victim could walk away before the moment of contact, spoiling the gag altogether.

Of course, executing this prank carried risks. There was no way to predict how a guest might react. Some folks have a grave fear of small, multi-legged creatures. Those who were victimized did not appreciate our brand of humor. Screaming at the sight of them was fairly common. But most people just jumped, then laughed it off.

Every so often a guest would complain to City Hall. Their level of discontent would become evident the following morning. Armed with scissors, supervisors would march into the shop and sever the strings that held up our creepy crawlers. All we could do is stand back and watch. But after keeping a low profile for a week or so, a fresh spool of string would appear and the spiders would resume their useful purpose.

Surprising guests in this way could sometimes be problematic. Ken Neufeld once landed a spider so softly on a woman's head that she didn't know it was there.

Raising it back up produced an unexpected result: the spider's rubbery legs had gotten tangled in the strands of her hair—only in this case, the hair was *not* her own. Inching the spider upward showed that she was wearing a wig. Thankfully, a few light tugs on the string freed the hairpiece. Unaware that an awkward moment had just been averted, the woman left the shop none the wiser.

Other issues that arose from deploying the spiders were not always physical. Sometimes it was the circumstances under which you chose to use them. I once faced such a situation:

It was a summer's night around closing time. As usual, the place was packed with shoppers, looking for that last-minute memento. In through the door marched an irate mother, whose two boys had come in to browse. She shouted at them loudly for all to hear, demanding they leave the shop "at once!" Every head turned toward the boisterous woman, with looks on their faces that said, "What's your problem, lady?" When the children did not obey their mother, the woman continued her tirade. Disneyland policy prohibited us from confronting ill-mannered guests. I could only hope that she would leave of her own accord. Only she didn't.

In a way I sympathized with her. The family had likely survived a long, hot day at Disneyland. Keeping tabs on a rambunctious brood under summertime conditions can unravel any parent's nerves.

But nothing was going to shut this woman up. There was, however, a remedy that wouldn't break any rules. By chance the brazen woman was standing right under the spider by the front door, and I was near the control string. I, alone, had the power to silence this obnoxious tyrant.

With only moments to launch my attack, there was no time for second thoughts. Down came the spider, landing right on the top of her head. A horrific scream, and out ran the frazzled mom.

As you can imagine, laughter filled the little shop. There might have even been applause, though not for me in particular. One advantage to being across the room is that it's hard to spot who had committed the prank. I was not going to be showered with praise for my bravery. But I did take satisfaction in one thing: no one laughed harder than those two boys.

In hindsight, humiliating that woman may not have been the best course of action. I had not only embarrassed her in front of her own children, but before a room full of strangers. I would like to think that the family had a good laugh about it on the way home. But even if they didn't, like all memories you take with you from a day at Disneyland, this one would surely remain for years to come. I could only hope that the mother reconciled the incident in the spirit in which it was intended. I later learned the result of my wishful thinking. I came to work the next day to find the spiders remanded to the supervisor's custody. Oh, well!

Love them or loathe them, over time the spiders developed a sort of fan base. I often saw guests come through the door and look up to see if they were still there.

As for our supervisors cutting them down, that was all part of the game. We were their disobedient children, and it was their duty to confiscate our toys whenever we misbehaved. Secretly, though, I think they enjoyed our zany antics as much as we did. I may have even detected a hint of envy in their eyes. But like Captain Hook, they controlled this corner of Never Land, and were assigned to enforce the rules. We were the Lost Boys of Main Street, and not yet ready to grow up.

So I've Been Told

Desk Set

It's not uncommon for personal relationships to develop in the workplace. Close collaboration between employees allows them to get more intimately acquainted, and before you know it, attachments are formed. Many will later find themselves kneeling at the altar at their own weddings. Similarly, romances have always flourished behind the scenes at Disneyland—and for good reason. Walt's early films consistently proclaimed that true love conquers all. Snow White would still be soundly asleep if not for that tender kiss from Prince Charming. Disneyland continues to promote that endearing sentiment throughout the park. Wherever guests go, a "happily ever after" awaits them around every corner. Former Magic Shop associate, Jim Turner, is more aware of this than anyone.

Like many Disneyland cast members in the 1970s, Jim worked there part-time while holding down his day job as a school teacher. He had gotten to know Claudia, the sweet girl who worked in the Tobacco Shop next door. By sheer coincidence, her younger brother was one of his junior high school students. He also knew her mother through PTA meetings, and had previously worked with her sister in Adventureland. That "Small World" he heard so many singing about was shrinking by the minute.

A series of shared lunch breaks, and the couple began dating. It didn't take long before Jim knew he wanted Claudia for his bride. She, however, wasn't sending out signals that she was ready for that commitment. Then one day, Jim returned to the shop from his break, when Jim Everett informed him: "Claudia called while you were out, and wanted to know where *'her man'* was." Shortly after, the betrothed Disneylanders announced their engagement!

The wedding date was set for June 18, 1976. The groom-to-be invited his Magic Shop buddies to attend. To make sure they all showed up, he proceeded to sear that date into their brains. "June 18th," he repeated often and endlessly. "Don't forget!" Normally, people mark their calendars to remember upcoming special events. But as you now know, the group running the Magic Shop was anything but normal. Jim was told to peek under the shopping bags that were stored below the counter. There, carved into the wooden shelf, was the date on which he would recite his wedding vows. No more annoying reminders were necessary after that.

Well, that glorious day arrived, and the Magic Shop contingent was on hand to wish Jim and Claudia all the best. After the ceremony ended and the reception guests had all gone home, the happy couple opened their wedding presents. Among them were comfy pillows for the living room and small appliances for the kitchen. Then they came upon a gift box tagged, *From your friends at the Main Street Magic Shop.* Unwrapping the box, the couple should have gasped at what they saw, but instead wiped away tears of delight. Inside was an office desk set. Glued to its base was a crudely sawed chunk of wood. Across it was etched the date, *June 18, 1976.* Jim's co-workers had secretly hacked out that piece of the Magic Shop counter to express their heartfelt congratulations.

While the newlyweds adored their surprise package, the gift-givers still faced some unfinished business. Their handiwork had left a huge hole in the Magic Shop counter. Luckily, someone had the foresight to draw up a template by tracing the removed section. A replacement piece was cut to size and epoxied into place. Applying shoe polish to the surface, the insert matched the stained shelf perfectly. Visit the Magic Shop today and you'll see those original counters still there. To my knowledge, evidence of that discreet modification remains undiscovered.

As for Jim Turner, he never forgets his wedding anniversary. That odd-looking desk set serves as a constant reminder of the happiest day he ever knew. His story further establishes that Disneyland was, and continues to be, fertile ground for relationships to grow. Over the years, many more like him would follow the sound of wedding bells, arm in arm with a fellow cast member . . . including me!

A piece of the Magic.

Chapter 7

The Bottom Line

"And there are pirates!"

—Peter Pan

I never saw a Profit and Loss Statement. There were no sales quotas to meet. No one worried about overhead costs or balance sheets. As with all retail stores, transactions were made and money changed hands. But none of us in the Magic Shop lost sleep over its fiscal health. We were artful conjurers, not financial wizards.

Simply put, the shop was a commercial enterprise. We sold goods to consumers. Product was ordered to fill the shelves through a supply chain, then shipped and delivered. In the morning you would slide open the door to stockroom 52H and there it would be, as if left overnight by the Tooth Fairy.

Once the shop doors were opened, our day-to-day duties weren't much different from that of any other marketplace. We rang cash registers—not the electronic kind you see today, but something much more primitive. We used the same Sweda machines you'd find in supermarkets of the day. Press a key and the sales figures spun around on rotating barrels—similar to old-style Vegas slot machines, but with numbers instead of fruit. Today's digital registers calculate the sales tax for you. We were afforded no such luxury. Taped to the corner of each digit were little numbered stickers. Tally them up to determine the tax, then add that amount to your total. It was fairly easy to do, and only a burden to those who couldn't add quickly in their heads when the shop got busy.

The bulk of our sales were made in the final hour before closing, amid the mad dash of guests making last-minute purchases. Summer nights were especially brutal. The shop would get so swamped that you barely had a moment to look away from the register keys. After a while you developed a rhythm of ringing, bagging, thanking the guest, then closing the register drawer. The only bottleneck was counting back change—something Cash Control insisted upon. (When's the last time a sales clerk did *that* for you?) But despite the pandemonium, you soldiered on.

While closing the shop was a test of endurance, opening it the next day was like waltzing into a cool, blue sunrise. Mornings were peaceful and slow. You listed the store items you needed to replenish, then wheeled a hand truck to the stockroom to retrieve them. This step was more crucial than you might think. Many times I started my afternoon shift to find the shelves nearly bare, all because someone neglected to pull stock that morning.

Like most all theme parks, Disneyland was not known for its discount pricing. Income from food and beverage sales, as well as merchandise, surely exceeded its earnings from selling admission tickets. You might then ask, Did the Magic Shop make money? That I couldn't say. I always just assumed that our totals were lumped in with all the other retail locations.

But whatever the park's profitability, selling Sponge Balls and Dribble Glasses certainly wasn't boosting Disneyland's bottom line. The one exception may have been our biggest-selling item: Spectaculars. These were giant sunglasses—an exaggerated version of what many like to associate with Hollywood glamour. They measured 12 inches across, and came in green or yellow. All around the park, guests could be seen wearing them proudly. In the summertime we sold so many that we stacked extra cartons behind the counter to avoid running out by day's end.

Social psychologists could surely shed light on why they were so popular. My theory is that deep inside, everyone is a closet comedian. Flaunting silly fashion accessories in public is our way of saying, "Hey, everyone! See how funny I am!" Those oversized shades more than fulfilled that desire, just as did its predecessor, the Invisible Dog Leash. But whatever the reason, it was a short-lived thrill. Guests returning home most certainly packed them away in a drawer, alongside their Mickey Mouse hats.

Ken Neufeld gleefully "pushes" the shop's
easy-to-learn magic tricks.

So, what was the real value of that item you just
bought at the Magic Shop? What did guests get for their
money? Not always what they expected. Take the classic
Cut and Restored Rope magic trick. For $2.75 you got a
length of "magicians" rope, bundled with printed instructions—essentially, a clothesline wrapped in paper.
There was nothing special about this rope. You probably
already owned one to hang your wet laundry on. If not,
you could buy one just like it at any hardware store for
pennies a foot. No, the value was not in the material.
What you paid for was to learn the secret to the trick!

Professor's Nightmare was another rope trick we sold. This one came with even less product: three pieces cut to various lengths. Not only did you get *less* rope, the quality of the packaging was also scaled down. It came in a standard business-size envelope, printed in one color. Other "envelope" tricks we offered included 2-card Monte and Glorpy the Gerkulating Ghost silk trick—all packaged in the cheapest way possible.

Again, you paid for the secret. We were not supposed to reveal what it was until after the trick had been paid for. I had a problem with this. I understood the product maker wanting to turn a profit. But withholding a trick's secret is a little like an abduction. No kidnapper would think of releasing his captive without *first* collecting the ransom.

So, what's to stop someone from buying a trick, learning its secret, then returning it for a refund? You can't exactly erase someone's memory as you hand them back their money. One solution made all that unnecessary: No refunds on magic! This was where I drew the line. Some tricks promised "no skill required." But according to whom? Everyone's capabilities are different. Most of the off-the-shelf tricks worked themselves with built-in gimmicks. All you had to do was memorize the patter. Others required greater manual dexterity. The multiplying Peter Rabbit trick looks easy, but requires more sleight of hand than you might think.

I never recommended a trick to anyone who didn't seem capable of doing it. For kids with little experience in magic, selling them something too advanced only invited frustration. I would see 8-year-olds watch one of us perform a complicated trick, unaware of how difficult it is. Then they'd buy it, only to find themselves unable to replicate what they had seen a professional do. So when a weepy-eyed child returned a trick because he couldn't make it work, I cheerfully gave him back his money. No questions asked.

The Magic Shop was a business. It thrived on generating sales. But I wasn't cut out to be a salesman. I never used high-pressure sales tactics, or did any of that "But wait!" stuff. I performed card tricks using a regular deck that most people already owned. Many walked in and walked out without spending a dime.

Is that anyway to run a store? Most assuredly not! But for guests who came there to see something amazing, I did my best not to disappoint them. And even though you can't take that to the bank, we're all a little richer for it.

MAGIC MOMENT
Jurassic Nonsense

With the Magic Shop's healthy sales volume, selling goods that were damaged or defective was inevitable. Oddly, customer returns were rare, considering how many of our imported items were so poorly made. Most of these were Joy Buzzers. The spring inside could only withstand so many turns, and over-tightening them caused it to snap. Black Soap was thin and brittle, and easily broke in half.

After refunding a guest's purchase, the rejected item was tossed into a box under the counter. Processing these "credits" was easy. When the box was full, you listed each item and its selling price on a standard form, then took it to a designated drop-off point. From there it was collected and taken to who knows where.

The collection sight nearest the Magic Shop was located inside the Primeval World Diorama building. Guests riding the Disneyland Railroad viewed this massive display of animated dinosaurs, in a prehistoric setting. A narrow alleyway behind it allowed maintenance crews to access the stage. We had been instructed to place our returned merchandise behind a chain link enclosure at the far end.

On one occasion, a co-worker and I entered the back door to drop off our box, when we suddenly heard the hissing of pneumatic cylinders. The mechanical creatures were coming to life, ahead of an approaching train. All was quiet otherwise. Only the train passengers heard the music and sound effects behind protective glass. Being an ardent fan of animatronics, I would love to have climbed up onto the platform to watch them up close. But who would explain to the guests what a 20th century man in a blue blazer was doing in the Cretaceous Period!

I bent down to place our box inside the enclosure. When I straightened up, my associate was gone. Then I spotted him. With no one else around, he did something I would never have the nerve to do. There he was, standing on the steps leading up to the stage. As the train chugged by, he poked his head up, just high enough to be visible to the train passengers. He stood there motionless, as if part of the scenery. I stood motionless watching him, frozen with disbelief.

The train finally exited through a tunnel, and the robot creatures fell silent once again. As my friend met me at the back door, I looked at him in astonishment.

"What?" he said, as if no one had ever done that before.

It's hard to know if anyone noticed the man peeking

over the toes of a Tyrannosaurus Rex. It's a huge display, with fog, swamps and erupting volcanoes. The size of his head would have been miniscule by comparison. If any guests had seen him, no one lodged a complaint. But then, why would anyone object to taking home a great Disneyland story like that?

MAGIC MOMENT
The Cola Spill
Challenge

I n the late 1970s, a cultural phenomenon was sweeping the nation known as the Cola Wars. Coke and Pepsi had both dominated the soft drink industry for nearly a century, yet neither wanted to be labeled as number 2. So began a marketing campaign that would place the Coca-Cola Company on notice, and see the rise of the "Pepsi Challenge" TV commercials.

The premise was simple: Displays were erected in shopping malls across the country, where average Americans were filmed participating in a blind taste test. Each was served a sample of two cola drinks—one Coke and one Pepsi. The cans from which each was poured were hidden from view. The participants were then asked to choose which one they liked better. The cans were uncovered. Predictably, each chose Pepsi.

We didn't sell beverages in the Magic Shop, but we did sell Coke and Pepsi cans. These were part of a line of "spill" gags. Some clever individual had found a way to make a plastic glob resemble a spilled soda drink. In the puddle lay an empty can on its side. Place it on a carpet or desktop and it appeared that the can had fallen over, spilling its contents onto the surface.

In keeping with the Magic Shop's reputation for silliness, we thought it might be fun to parody those commercials. We laid one each of the Coke and Pepsi spills on the counter, then covered the cans with a box, leaving only the spills exposed. The writing on the box posed the question, "Which is Pepsi?" Of course, each spill looked exactly alike, giving you an even chance of getting it right. After guests made their selection, their choice was revealed. It was not our intention to endorse either soda product. It was just an entertaining piece of handmade nonsense that never failed to get a laugh.

We further expanded on this theme with two other kinds of spills. Gooey Humor looked like a half-melted ice cream bar, with its wooden stem still attached. Similar to the soda gags, the Chocolate Syrup Spill mimicked a glob of chocolate sauce. Like before, the source of the mess was covered with a box. The question now being asked was, "Which is Bosco?" Guests played along as before for the fun of it.

But when word of this latest challenge reached our supervisors, we were immediately told to cease and desist. The reason for this is still unclear. One possibility was that they feared our use of brand names might constitute trademark infringement. The other was that we were being racially insensitive. A popular non-Disney cartoon character from the 1920s named Bosko (with a "k") was being confused with the ice cream topping Bosco (with a "c"). Bosko the cartoon resembled a black-faced minstrel show performer, and spoke with a stereotypical Southern drawl. None of us had heard of this character, nor did we ever imagine that our little contest might be politically incorrect. But whatever had caused this backlash, our little parody came to an abrupt end, and the spills went back to being a mediocre prank.

Chapter 8

The Routine

"Children have the strangest adventures
without being troubled by them."

—Wendy

Being a Disneyland cast member wasn't all dream castles and tiki birds. It was work, too. You followed company protocol just like you would in any other job. Disneyland had a huge number of employees, so enforcing a reasonable amount of discipline was necessary. The rules were not terribly stringent, but not playing by them brought consequences.

The official guidelines kicked in the moment you showed up for work. Employee parking was located just outside the park's perimeter, alongside Harbor Blvd. Lots were marked "A" for close-up parking, and "X" marked the spaces furthest from the cast member entrance. Early shifters were required to park in the distant section, allowing those arriving later to occupy close-up spaces—a system I never quite understood. Certainly the latecomers were just as capable of walking that longer distance.

You clocked in 15 minutes before the start of your

shift, allowing you time to get into costume. If you punched in late, you were docked a quarter-hour's pay. Those who were required to park their cars in the furthermost parking lot needed to allow extra time to reach the time shack. Sometimes those who were running late, and riding with another cast member, would drop their passenger off at the curb. While the driver parked the car, the other would punch you both in to avoid being penalized. This was breaking the rules. Anyone caught engaging in this devious practice was in deep trouble. Keeping a sharp eye out for Security was essential when committing this loathsome act.

At the end of your shift, clocking out *early* also meant getting a leaner paycheck. It took me a while to figure out why I was only getting paid for 7.75 hours of work when I knew I worked 8. This also explained why I saw people huddled around the time clock, waiting for it to reach the top of the hour before punching out.

How much you earned per hour varied depending on which department you worked in. Operations workers were paid the best. Merchandise Hosts, not so much. People in Foods occupied the bottom rung of the pay scale ladder. Some positions required you to join a union. I belonged to the Retail Clerks Union Local 324, which provided some earnings and benefit security. Even so, my weekly paycheck was meager by today's standards. I've always found it amazing how I lived so comfortably on such a small amount. But back then, my studio apartment only cost me $300 a month!

DISNEYLAND, ANAHEIM, CA.			ORD DY/WKY						C047835 337191	
EMPLOYEE NAME			SOCIAL SECURITY NO.	ORIGIN	DEPT.	LOCATION	W9	PAY PERIOD	WEEK ENDING	
BRUCE A EDWARDS				02	912	546	34	36	09/02/78	

COMPUTATION OF GROSS			MISCELLANEOUS DEDUCTIONS		TAXES	
DESCRIPTION	HOURS	EARNINGS	UNION DUES	8.00	FEDERAL INCOME	12.57
STRAIGHT TIME	40.0	195.75			FEDERAL INSURANCE CONTRIBUTION ACT	11.84
					STATE DISABILITY INSURANCE	1.96
					STATE INCOME	1.32
					CITY INCOME	
					TOTAL:	27.69
					YEAR TO DATE TOTALS	
					GROSS	2312.62
					FEDERAL INCOME TAX	26.44
					FEDERAL INSURANCE CONTRIBUTION ACT	139.91
TOTAL GROSS:	40.0	195.75			STATE DISABILITY INSURANCE	23.13
TOTAL DEDUCTIONS & TAXES:		35.69			STATE INCOME TAX	1.85
NET PAY:		160.06	WEEKLY TOTAL:	8.00	CITY INCOME TAX	

Adequate income.

In some situations you were paid extra to provide services over and above your job description. The Magic Shop had its own bonus structure. If you were the designated "magic demo," your pay rate increased. At least one magic demonstrator was required to be on duty at all times. One summer, a 4-hour gap between the time the morning demo person went home and the nighttime one came on, left me in charge of demonstrating tricks. During those 4 hours each day, my pay zoomed to top rate, in addition to that coveted demo pay!

To further augment my income, I volunteered for the "A/B draw." This allowed supervisors to borrow hosts from one land, to fill position shortages in another. I was called upon to work in Tomorrowland's Character Shop, which carried an array of novelty items, each with a futuristic theme. I was given the chore of folding t-shirts —not a difficult task, but one that turned out to be agonizingly frustrating. My job was to stand in front of the display and keep it neat. What I didn't expect was the flood of guests, each holding up shirts to examine the fit, then tossing them back down in a heap. Before I knew it, my immaculate display looked like the discount bin at an outlet store. Hour after hour, my folded shirts were snatched up, then discarded, whereupon I folded them again! The next day I begged to return to my post in the Magic Shop.

Being a "lead" also got you an extra something in your paycheck. These employees served as mini bosses for each area. One of their responsibilities was scheduling breaks and lunches. You were allowed two 15-minute breaks per shift. Lunchtime lasted 30 minutes. The exact time when breaks were assigned was not rigorously enforced. If you were nice to your lead, she might be persuaded to arrange it so that you and your buddies could have lunch together. I took advantage of this one night to see Buddy Rich and His Big Band perform on the Carnation Gardens stage. Buddy had been my idol since I was a 12-year-old wannabe drummer. I had hoped to catch his last set, but to my dismay, Buddy had been forced to quit early. Visibly perturbed, he announced to his audience, "Sorry, folks, I have to stop on account of some cockamamie parade!"

Your lunchtime meal could be whatever you wanted, with one caveat: you could not go off site to eat it. Walking into a Burger King dressed as a cartoon dwarf was not permitted. Unless you brought your own food, you had your choice of two backstage cafeterias. One was named The Inn Between, located "between" Main

Street and Tomorrowland. Most cast members working nearby preferred dining there. The other was named the DEC (Disneyland Employee Cafeteria), which was hidden below New Orleans Square. Disneylanders more often referred to it as "The Pit"—its original name before cast members voted to change it.

For a quick bite, backstage patio areas offered vending machines with a selection of snacks. In the summer months, the benches became rest stops for the walk-around characters, trying to recover from the often blistering Southern California heat. I met a lot of interesting people back there, like Paul Castle, who had worn the Mickey Mouse costume since the 1960s, often standing alongside Walt Disney on photo shoots. I became friends with Harry Brice, Main Street's legendary silhouette cutter, whom I discovered was an equally talented cartoonist.

Standing in the shadow of Space Mountain was The Center. This portable office trailer had a functioning Bank of America inside, affectionately nicknamed Mickey's Mint. There you could cash your paycheck, hold meetings in its conference room, or lounge in a comfortable chair while sipping a cup of free coffee. This air-conditioned space was greatly appreciated in the summertime. It was not uncommon to see sweat-drenched Disney characters endorsing their payroll checks.

One *unofficial* onstage duty involved admitting park visitors. Before the creation of the Annual Pass, visiting Disneyland on a regular basis required a significant investment. But there was one way to get in for free: ask a cast member to sign you in. Since the Magic Shop was close to the Main Gate entrance, we were often called upon to provide this service. The phone would ring, and someone way out in Critter Country might ask you for the favor. The Magic Shop had its own regulars who we routinely signed in. Some were Magic Castle members we knew, like the Gray Line Bus Tour driver who hung out with us, while his passengers roamed the park. Magicians from our rival magic shop at Knott's Berry Farm were always welcome. We were only supposed to admit people we knew, but we typically overlooked that restriction. One old guy in particular had been coming there every day for years. He was a stranger to me, but I allowed him entry anyway. Again, this was against the rules, but in this case, no one had the heart to enforce it.

The arrival of each season brought its own set of responsibilities. Summer nights saw the return of the Main Street Electrical Parade. While guests lined the street waiting for it to arrive, some of us were recruited to provide crowd control. We helped guests cross the street and made sure they stayed behind the roped-off perimeter. To a magician, these weren't just parade goers, they were a captive audience. When my turn came to keep these people in line, those who obeyed my instructions were rewarded with a magic trick.

Each Christmas, Disneyland hosted its annual Candlelight Procession. Hundreds of carolers, each carrying a candle, slow-marched down Main Street toward the train station, where they sang with a live orchestra. The lights on Main Street were dimmed to heighten the candlelight effect. Those wishing to bypass the sidewalk observers were ushered through the shops. Flashlights were used to help guide them through the darkness. In true Magic Shop fashion, we safely guided guests with the help of "Atomic Lamps"—light bulbs that lit up when you held them in your hand.

Working Grad Nites presented its own unique challenges. This was when late-night bus-loads of graduating high school students took over the park, partying till dawn the next morning. As the teenage revelers enjoyed Disneyland's more exhilarating attractions, Main Street remained mostly deserted. The first hurtle was struggling to stay awake till the wee hours. During those long stretches of inactivity, we busied ourselves by dusting shelves and tidying up. As the evening wore on, you began to get punchy. A wandering guest would occasionally stroll in to see a trick. The end of each event brought the usual all-out shopper assault. If you hadn't caught your second wind by then, you were in for a rude awakening.

Whatever the season, your supervisors kept track of how well you performed your duties. If mistakes were made, a conversation usually smoothed out any rough spots. But if you were called up to your bosses office, you had screwed up royally! Throughout the year, all your bungles, the big and the small, were noted. Then came what every working person in the world dreads: the annual performance appraisal.

In my earlier days I received excellent marks, praised for being courteous and knowledgeable:

Bruce Edwards
Merchandise Host
North Merchandise, Dept. 921
July 14, 1979

"Bruce has done an excellent job as a Merchandise Host this past year. He is very dependable and hard working. Not only is his guest courtesy excellent, his working relationships are also very good. He seems to enjoy his work and this enjoyment spreads to the guests and his fellow employees. They enjoy being around him. His knowledge of the Magic Shop is excellent and he is quite willing to help out in any way necessary. Overall, Bruce is quite an asset to the shop and to the area."

In 1980, I drew up a lesson plan for a Magic Shop class which included instruction on how to perform simple tricks. This assured that any Main Street Host assigned to the shop would have the know-how to execute something magical if asked. All cast members were invited to attend the voluntary sessions. The 2-day course only demanded 15 minutes in the morning before starting work. But somehow this well-intentioned effort did not translate into a positive review:

Bruce Edwards
Merchandise Host
North Merchandise, Dept. 921
August 21, 1980

"Bruce did very well when presenting a Magic class at the beginning of summer. The class was a two-day presentation and Bruce wrote a manual to go along with the class. Bruce still needs to work on his attitude, because it seems to fluctuate at times, and this fluctuation seems to affect his working relationship with his leads. Bruce has below average presenteeism and needs to show improvement in this area. Overall, Bruce is above average as an employee when he doesn't allow his attitude to effect his job performance."

Seeing my questionable attitude stated so explicitly was a total shock. I had initiated the Magic Shop class on my own. Surely that would earn me a stellar evaluation. But the criticism was undoubtedly justified. The pixie dust that had sustained me all those years was wearing off. I felt the daily grind closing in on me, like the *tick-tock* of Captain Hook's crocodile. I was little more than a cog in a machine, albeit one designed to manufacture fantasy and inspiration.

I wasn't the only cast member to feel that way. The positive vibe that enshrouded Disneyland was waning. The parent company outside Walt's park was changing, too. Roy E. Disney, Walt's nephew and Disney Company board member, had already resigned his executive post over the company's diminishing product quality. In a few short years, control over Disneyland would fall into more risk-averse hands. For me, that magical pot of gold had simply played out.

MAGIC MOMENT
Fun with Mr. Lincoln

Disneyland's normal operating day had ended. Leaving the Magic Shop, I walked past the backstage entrance to the Main Street Opera House, better known as the home of Great Moments with Mr. Lincoln. The doors stood open, and a truck parked nearby had the word *Animation* painted across it. I thought, What were animators doing inside the Mr. Lincoln attraction? It turns out that the department was responsible for maintaining the animatronic characters throughout the park.

I poked my head in through the door to see the robot president, silently standing and sitting repeatedly. Then he would raise one arm, then the other. Chatting with a technician, I learned that Mr. Lincoln was running in "test mode." This enabled the crew to diagnose his overall robotic health, and ward off any potential mechanical hiccups.

I introduced myself as a Main Street Magic Shop

magician, and confessed my fascination with animatronics. I was invited up onto the stage to examine Mr. Lincoln more closely. Standing next to the world-famous figure was like being near a celebrity. I looked into his eyes, as if expecting him to look back and say, How y'all doin'? If not for the zipper on the back of his rubber neck, he looked astonishingly human. But that was the whole idea. For an audience to accept the dignity of the presentation, they had to suspend their disbelief that he was only a machine.

I learned just how believable he really was through a most unlikely source:

In those days, Disneyland was closed Mondays and Tuesdays, and on certain evenings, cast members were treated to a family film festival. A selection of Disney movies were shown in the Lincoln Theatre. The films were projected onto a screen that hung in front of the onstage character. At one screening, I brought my young son along to see the animated classic *Lady and the Tramp*. The evening ended, and while people filed out of the theater, we stayed behind to chat with friends.

As the theater crew prepared the attraction for the next day, the movie screen was raised. Slumped over in his chair sat Mr. Lincoln, his power source shut off. I then made a tasteless remark about the former president having been shot. All the way home, my son was unusually quiet. When I asked him what was wrong, he belittled me for being so mean, distraught that I had made light over the death of that dear man he perceived as being real.

Watching Mr. Lincoln continue with his diagnostic program, I learn some fascinating facts. As he began to sit down, the technician suddenly pulled his chair away. I momentarily reached out as a warning that he might fall down. To my amazement, the president floated above the floor, as if assisting a magician in a levitation act. He had been designed not to rely on his chair for support.

Then the technician reached into the wings and brought out a straw hat—not a skimmer like the Main Street Dapper Dans wore, but the Tom Sawyer variety. As the mechanical president went through his motions, he placed it on his head. I hesitated before laughing, fearing he had committed a kind of sacrilege. Then I realized that I was observing that same goofiness that went on every day in the Magic Shop.

The following night, the Animation team returned to continue calibrating Mr. Lincoln. I stopped by for another visit, this time carrying a pair of Beagle Puss glasses we sold in the shop. These are more commonly referred to as "Groucho" glasses: wide frames with a large rubber nose and mustache attached to it. As I presented the technician with the classic disguise, he didn't hesitate to place it on the bridge of Mr. Lincoln's nose.

Some might regard dishonoring this Disneyland icon as unconscionable. Don't get me wrong. Great Moments with Mr. Lincoln is one of my all-time favorite attractions. Listening to his stirring speech never fails to put a lump in my throat. But there is something in human nature that demands we show our silly side every once in a while. It's perfectly reasonable to assume that Mr. Lincoln's developers did much the same thing. There were certainly opportunities to put a flower behind his ear or a beer bottle in his hand.

Whether behind Mr. Lincoln's back, or the Magic Shop counter, we all look for ways to make the world a little more fun to be in. Walt may not have approved of me disrespecting his creation. But when he initially proposed building Disneyland, his critics responded, Are you joking? The media labeled his pet project "Walt's folly," fully expecting it to fail. Walt Disney would ultimately have the last laugh, as his dream evolved into a worldwide phenomenon. He understood the value of a healthy sense of humor. And if scholars of American history are correct, honest Abe Lincoln was a bit of a funnyman himself.

Magician Mark Neynaber demonstrates the
proper use of Beagle Puss glasses.

Chapter 9

Fade Out

"Oh, why can't you remain like this forever?"
—Mrs. Darling

Passing through the gates of Disneyland is like walking onto a movie set. Each land tells its own cinematic story. Journey through an African jungle in Adventureland. Travel back to a time of wilderness forts in Frontierland. Cast members fill the roles necessary to bring these stories to life. From fearless jungle boat skippers to voluptuous saloon gals, each part they play is essential.

But Disneyland is a movie without an ending. It continues on, and yet, not so for its cast of characters. For many, the park merely serves as a stepping stone to the future. Graduating students leave to pursue their chosen professions. Others venture off to explore broader horizons. Most of the Magic Shop magicians had already moved on. And as they departed, the demand from guests to "Do a trick!" began to fade. Now I was facing that same crossroad.

In my struggle to decide whether to leave, an unforeseen

incident made up my mind for me. I had arrived to work late, and rather than park my car in lot X, I steered around the orange traffic cones and chose a close-up space. A security guard saw what I had done and confronted me. I smiled, and joked that this was not a habit with me. "It'll never happen again," I quipped.

But he didn't smile back. He demanded I move my car. Normally, I tend to avoid confrontation, but I asked him what would happen if I refused. He answered,

"Then I will confiscate your ID card!"

"What if I don't give it to you?"

"Then you'll be charged with possession of stolen property!" More threats of retaliation followed if I did not comply.

I wasn't playing by the book, and I knew it. I respected the security guard for fulfilling his sworn duty. What bothered me was the complete absence of that Disney good-naturedness. Not that I was any better. That bad attitude I had been warned about had surfaced without me knowing it. I should have given the guard an "awe, shucks!" for getting busted and honored his request. And while I held no grudges, the writing was on the wall. The time had come for me to go my own way. I moved my car, got into costume, then climbed the steps to the Main Street office and graciously tendered my resignation.

My final day as a cast member still haunts me. Disneyland had already closed on a warm summer's evening. The floats of the Electrical Parade lay quiet in a darkened storehouse. As the crowds thinned out, I counted the change in my cash drawer. Cash Control came in to "Z out" my register—an operation that resets the machine for the next day. I took a few minutes to clean up behind the counter. Then I grabbed my money bag, turned out the lights, and locked the doors to the Magic Shop for the last time.

Main Street was now empty, just like I had seen it the first day I arrived. I glanced up at the rooftop lights, and thought, This is the last thing people see before leaving Disneyland. A kind of quiet serenity hangs in the air. It's a place for folks to decompress after a long day of standing in lines, keeping the kids together and diapering the baby. Families rejoin their loved ones in Town Square after one last ride on Space Mountain. And as they head toward the exit gate, they sense these parting words: Thanks for coming. I hope you enjoyed your stay. The park was saying good-by to me, too, with a note of thanks for playing a small role in the Disneyland story.

Backstage, I turned in my blue blazer, passing it on to the next long-armed recruit. I went to my locker and transformed back into an average Joe. I clocked out, and was a Disneyland cast member no more.

It's hard to predict just how the choices we make will impact our lives. I had applied for work at Disneyland out of necessity. It was a move of no great significance —a passing note in a musical arrangement. How long I would remain there never crossed my mind. I was a summer wage-earner, nothing more. How could I have anticipated what adventures awaited me there? To this day, the Magic Shop continues to influence what I do and how I act. I pick up a deck of cards and instinctively hold them in the default position, ready to double-lift the top card or "deal seconds" should the need arise. I'm always ready to perform my favorite vanishing coin trick whenever I dine out with friends.

I continued to associate with most of my fellow cast members. Silhouette artist Harry Brice and I co-developed a multimedia stage show, for a nonprofit that promoted child safety. Harry took care of the visuals. I produced the audio/video portion. Former Disneyland entertainers performed the song and dance numbers live on stage. And before each show I warmed up our young audiences with a magic trick or two.

Magic Shop colleague Harry Snowden and I created a Muppet-style hand puppet that performed magic. Harry operated the head and mouth, while my hands protruded from its sleeves to do close-up tricks. Manfred the Magic Puppet could be seen at Adventure City's Puppet Center, just down the road from Knott's Berry Farm.

On a more professional level, I was commissioned to compose and record a variety of radio jingles. I contracted musicians I had played with in the past, including my brother Bob on keyboards. While we all lent our singing voices, two additional singers added a little magic to the vocal tracks. Mark Neynaber and Ken Neufeld, both talented musicians in their own right, expertly sang lead and backup vocals on the recording dates.

Fortune also smiled on my personal life. My childhood dream of becoming an animator came true, working for the big Hollywood studios, including Warner Bros. Feature Animation and Fox Animation Studios. Computer animators were in high demand then, thanks to Disney's runaway success with its Toy Story movies.

And if that weren't enough, that Disneyland love bug that caused so many relationships to flourish had bitten me, too. I married my backstage sweetheart shortly after leaving the company.

I still live in Orange County, just a short drive from Disneyland. The motel where I stayed in 1957 still stands, though now dwarfed by an overabundance of high-rise luxury hotels. The skyline of the park has also changed considerably. New and taller structures now reach high into the skies over Anaheim. But there's still no mistaking Matterhorn Mountain. Whenever I see it towering above the trees that once shielded orange groves, I think of that wide-eyed 12-year-old.

The old Magic Shop gang still gets together every now and then for mini reunions. There we reminisce about the people we worked with and recall stories of snakes in cans and spiders on strings. It's a rare group of individuals, who ushered in the golden age of the Main Street Magic Shop.

Several years passed before I returned to Disneyland as a guest. Stopping by the Magic Shop on Main Street, I was disheartened to find that souvenirs had taken over much of the shelf space. I couldn't find a single person to show me a trick, not even the Chinese Sticks. I would gladly have settled for a Ball and Vase demonstration. Not until 2009 would the shop regain the distinction of being a house of magic, when retailer Houdini Magic leased the space.

As much as I hate to say this, Magic is fake. Most professional magicians openly admit that. Watching someone vanish a coin can be mystifying, but it's just an illusion. Common sense tells us that solid objects can't vanish into thin air, no more than a sprinkling of pixie dust can make you fly. But even the laws of physics are called into question when watching a really good magician. I've always thought of the Magic Shop that way. It was an odd-shaped, little room with no magical properties, and yet, it defied logic by making me feel like a kid again.

But that was long ago. Today I bear the responsibilities that come with adulthood. Not a week goes by without some new global crisis to worry about. I'm a citizen of the *real* world now, just like Wendy and the Lost Boys became when they left Never Land for good. In a strange way, I took that journey with them. I followed my curiosity to an enchanted land in search of adventure, then returned home in order that others might enjoy the same experience.

It's been said that youth is a state of mind. As I grow older, I wonder if that's true. One needs only to fly to that island in the clouds to find the answer. Too bad I'm all out of pixie dust. But maybe I don't need it. On a warm summer's night, I'll follow that second star to the right to a theme park in Anaheim. Then I'd gaze into that little shop on Main Street, and with the full moon in my eyes, ask, "Is this the way to Never Land?"

Main Street Magic Shop reunion, 2017.

Back: Jim Everett, Karen Everett, Christy Sims Neynaber,
Bruce Edwards, Mark Neynaber, Bobbie Menn Tier,
Bill Diemert.

Front: Ken Neufeld, Chuck Lucas, Jim Turner.

About the Author

Bruce Edwards was born in Marin County, California and raised on a tasty diet of Jazz and Disney animation. He majored in Architecture in college, then switched to Music to join the burgeoning San Francisco music scene. As a composer and musician, he wrote rock tunes and radio jingles, and toured as a pop music artist. Tinkering with early computer animation led to a career as a feature film character animator. He wrote screenplays during his Hollywood years before finding an audience for his young-adult fiction. His more unusual vocational detours include a stint as a puppeteer and designing and building animatronic characters. Bruce lives in Orange County, California.

Learn more about Bruce and discover his other book titles at

BruceEdwardsBooks.com

Sources

Barrie, J.M. *Peter and Wendy*. Scribner, 1911.

Hendler, Kari. "Disneyland's Main Street Magic: the Magic Inside the Kingdom." *Magic Magazine,* July, 2015.

Thomas, Bob. *Walt Disney: An American Original.* Hyperion, 1976, 1995.

"Mastering the Tricks of Their Trade." *Disneyland Line.* Cast member newsletter, July 22, 1977.

Martin, Steve. *Born Standing Up: A Comic's Life.* Scribner, 2007.

www.TheEdwardsBrothers.com

Photos courtesy of Bill Diemert, Bob Edwards and other Disneyland cast members.

Cover design by Bruce Edwards.

The author wishes to acknowledge these former Disneylanders for their help in verifying the accuracy of this book's contents:
Ken Neufeld, Chuck Lucas, Jim Turner, Jim Everett, Mark Neynaber, Harry Snowden, and Jacki Edwards.

Continue the Adventure!

Video
Bonus Stories
Trivia
Photo Gallery

BruceEdwardsBooks.com/magic

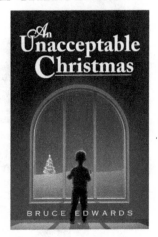

BONEHEAD BOOTCAMP

Book #1

Amy is unjustly sent to a boot camp for troubled teens.

"Truly a book about finding one's real self."

—*All Books Review*

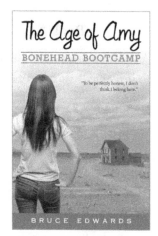

ISBN: 9780983760403

THE THUMPER AMENDMENT

Book #2

Amy joins a presidential campaign to get even with a grade school bully.

"Readers will appreciate Amy's sharp wit."

—*Booklist*

ISBN: 9780983760429

CHANNEL '63

Book #3

Amy finds love through a TV that receives signals from 1963.

"A riotous young-adult adventure."

—*Foreword Reviews*

ISBN: 9780983760443

BEHIND THE FUN ZONE

Book #4

Amy takes on Silicon Valley when device-addicted teens start disappearing.

"An unfailingly entertaining read from beginning to end."

—*Midwest Book Review*

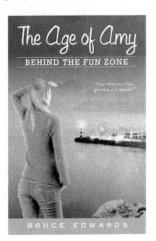

ISBN: 9780983760467

MADDOGS AND MAKEOVERS

Book #5

A late-night phone call from a stranger implicates Amy in a terrorist plot.

> "Head and shoulders above most in this genre."
>
> —*Readers' Favorite*

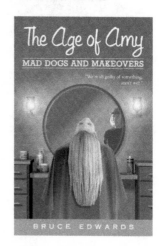

ISBN: 9780983760498

THE COMPLETE SERIES

5-book Box Set

- Bonehead Bootcamp
- The Thumper Amendment
- Channel '63
- Behind the Fun Zone
- Mad Dogs and Makeovers

ISBN: 9780692890752

9 781737 428503